WORSHIP, WIN
URBAN C.

WORSHIP,
WINDOW OF THE
URBAN CHURCH

Edited by

TIM STRATFORD

First published in Great Britain in 2006

Society for Promoting Christian Knowledge
36 Causton Street
London SW1P 4ST

British Library Cataloguing-in-Publication Data
A catalogue record for this book is available from the British Library

ISBN-13: 978–0–281–05783–2
ISBN-10: 0–281–05783–4

1 3 5 7 9 10 8 6 4 2

Typeset by Graphicraft Ltd, Hong Kong
Printed in Great Britain by Ashford Colour Press

Contents

Contents

Contributors

John Austin has recently retired after thirteen years as the Suffragan Bishop of Aston in Birmingham where he was heavily involved in regeneration initiatives both within the Church and in the city, and was the Chair of the City Challenge Board from 1993 to 1999. He was also deeply involved in interfaith matters, chairing the Inter Faith Consultative Group of General Synod and the joint Christian Muslim group which made the proposals leading to the formation of the Christian Muslim Forum for England.

Erica Dunmow has lived and worshipped in multicultural inner-city and estate churches for the past 25 years, in local ecumenical partnerships, including Anglican, Baptist, Catholic, Methodist and United Reformed traditions. Although a Methodist by background and a serving local preacher, she actively draws upon all those traditions, and charismatic practice, in leading and developing new forms of worship: the main focus of her MA. She is currently Urban Mission Development Advisor for a churches and mission agencies project (funding comes from the Evangelical Coalition for Urban Mission and the Methodist Church) serving the UK.

Kathy Galloway is the Leader of the Iona Community and lives in Glasgow. She is a practical theologian, campaigner and writer. She is the author or editor of 14 books of theology, liturgy and poetry, and her writings have been widely anthologized.

After **Ann Jeffries** took early retirement from the University of Plymouth, where she had taught Community and Social Work for 16 years, she was appointed as Community Development Advisor to the Anglican Bishop of Plymouth's Advisory Group. Ann's earlier experiences also included community social work in inner-city areas in Michigan, USA, where she was also involved in church-based social action in support of the Black Civil Rights Movement.

Canon Dr Graham Kings became the Vicar of Islington, at St Mary's Church, in 2000. He is a member of the Liturgical Commission, the Theological Secretary of Fulcrum and was previously the founding

Director of the Henry Martyn Centre for the study of mission and world Christianity in the Cambridge Theological Federation and vice-principal of St Andrew's College, Kabare, Kenya.

Ann Morisy is Commission Officer for the Commission on Urban Life and Faith (CULF). She has worked for many years alongside churches as they engage with their communities. Ann is the author of two best-sellers: *Beyond the Good Samaritan* and more recently, *Journeying Out.*

Tim Stratford has been Team Rector of the Kirkby Team Ministry on the north-east edge of Liverpool since 2003. He is a member of the General Synod and a member of the 2006–10 Liturgical Commission. He has served for 12 years in outer-estate Church of England parishes, partly inspired by his three years as chaplain to David Sheppard, a former Bishop of Liverpool.

John Vincent founded the Urban Theology Unit in Sheffield in 1969, and edited the Methodist Report, *The Cities* (1997) and the St Deiniol's Report, *Faithfulness in the City* (2003). He is also a New Testament scholar, and edited the recent SPCK collection, *Mark: Gospel of Action* (2006).

Martin Wallace is now Bishop of Selby. He has also been the chaplain of a seventh-century Celtic chapel and has compiled *Pocket Celtic Prayers.*

Mark Waters is an Anglican priest who has worked in full-time parish ministry and in sector ministries in the areas of social responsibility and community organizing. He currently works for Church Action on Poverty developing a programme of work around citizen participation. His church base is as a non-stipendiary curate in the United Benefice of St Faith, Crosby and St Mary, Waterloo in Liverpool.

Acknowledgements

The editor gratefully acknowledges permission to reproduce the following extracts:

Martin Wallace, *City Prayers*, Norwich: Canterbury Press, 1995.
George MacLeod, *Only One Way Left*, Glasgow: Iona Community, 1956.

Kathy Galloway acknowledges permission to use the following:

'How Long, O Lord?' and 'Inspired by Love and Anger' from *Heaven Shall Not Wait* (Glasgow: Wild Goose Publications, 1987), text by John L. Bell and Graham Maule, copyright © 1987 WGRG, Iona Community, Glasgow G2 3DH, Scotland. Reproduced by permission.

'Don't Tell Me of a Faith that Fears' from *Enemy of Apathy* (Glasgow: Wild Goose Publications, 1988), text by John L. Bell and Graham Maule, copyright © 1988 WGRG, Iona Community, Glasgow G2 3DH, Scotland. Reproduced by permission.

'I Shall Praise You, O Lord, from My Soul' from *Psalms of Patience, Protest and Praise* (Glasgow: Wild Goose Publications, 1993), text by John L. Bell, copyright © 1993 WGRG, Iona Community, Glasgow G2 3DH, Scotland. Reproduced by permission.

'God Asks, "Who Will Go for Me?"' from the song 'Inspired by Love and Anger', as quoted above.

Preface

TIM STRATFORD

The metaphor of worship as a window is well worn. A former Archbishop of Canterbury once described worship as the Church's shop window. Others have described worship as a window into the very Kingdom of God. In this book we will be exploring how worship lends insight to the people of God in a very active way. This is no mere window that you can gaze in through and walk away from. Here we describe worship that changes perceptions. We would have preferred to write of worship as a lens, imagining a camera for which this is a critical transforming component. The use, placement and settings of a lens determine a scene's final interpretation but that metaphor was too complex to carry on a book's covers. These active aspects of worship forming and transforming those who engage in it is not lost, however, though the idea of worship as a window perhaps also reminds us of how it frames and makes transparent the interaction of human beings with God in our world.

Our focus is on exploring and demonstrating how our faith tradition encourages and facilitates a deep literacy and understanding of the world; a literacy that has been formed through spiritual struggle and collective learning. Another way of saying this is 'a different way of doing audit'. That is, looking at ourselves and the world through the window of prayer, worship, ritual, shared experience and Scripture.

We write from an urban perspective but not exclusively to any particular urban context. We hope that the thinking and experience described here will be a good contribution to debate as *Faithful Cities*, the report of the Commission on Urban Life and Faith, is digested by a wide-ranging set of people.

Our use of 'urban' as a term here is not a particularly limited or technical one. We are aware that urban contexts range from among the world's poorest communities to the world's very richest. This is as true of the British urban scene as it is anywhere else. Furthermore, urban contexts are not all in or around cities nor are they all multicultural and cosmopolitan. A plurality of these settings is represented here.

It had originally been our brief to include writing from other faith traditions. That was not easy to do in the end, either because of this editor's inexperience or because the notion that worship changes perceptions and actions carried most resonance in the Christian Church, or for some other more complex reason. Understandings of what worship is about vary greatly across the Churches as well as between the faiths. We hope the insights here will enrich that understanding.

We have deliberately set out to write a book with some integrity between the chapters, notwithstanding our varied backgrounds. Twenty-four hours in which most of our contributors were able to meet and come to terms with each other's ideas was invaluable. We hope the sparks and relationships that this generated are evident in our texts.

Now, if I may extend the metaphor we have adopted, our work is divided into three parts:

- worship as a window into the Kingdom of God;
- worship as a window into human faith;
- worship as a window into the patterns of our world.

Windows into the Kingdom

In Part 1, the first three contributions by Bishop John Austin, Kathy Galloway and John Vincent discuss the nature of worship. In Chapter 1, John Austin begins with the processes of regeneration and the determination to form 'flourishing communities' that dominate much urban activity in Britain at present. He asks a question about where values come from. At the heart of his values lies a realization of the forgiveness of God as definitive. He opens up a number of questions about how Christian values that contribute towards flourishing communities are represented in our formal and informal worship.

In Chapter 2, Kathy Galloway leads us on to reflect that worship is an alien activity to many today. We do indeed 'sing the Lord's song in a strange land'. She describes worship as a counter-cultural and re-defining activity, voicing pain, acknowledging sin, ridiculing power and expressing defiance. These things belong to the Kingdom.

This contribution is a light revision of a presentation she made to the National Estate Churches Network. At that event the poetic lines were sung. Some readers may want to have a go at singing the words to themselves – most might not dare.

In Chapter 3, John Vincent offers a number of 'people's liturgies' that have grown out of small communities. These belong to very particular contexts in which they have been honed and refined. They are illustrative of the nature of worship in interdenominational or postdenominational missionary urban contexts. Their existence challenges churches that regulate or authorize particular forms of worship and begs the question about whether a one-size-fits-all approach limits our vision of the Kingdom. His description of the context that his liturgies have grown out of helps reinforce the importance of our localness in our relation with God.

Windows into Faith

In Part 2, the next three contributions describe worship that involves risk. This leads to places that the Church and its members will be unable to go without a sense of faith and adventure. Martin Wallace in Chapter 4 describes such worship as not being about pushing God's finger to point where we think it should but as sitting on the finger of God to see where he is pointing. The image of a roller coaster is perhaps not inappropriate.

The two Anns (Morisy and Jeffries) in Chapter 5 urge Christian people to seize the moment in creating apt liturgies. Without re-quiring that people cross the threshold of a church, they urge the faithful to bring their hopes and fears before God in the ordinary public places where daily life is worked out. Moments when people may be ready to respond to this might often be quite small. Graham Kings goes on in Chapter 6 to describe how his church in the heart of Islington takes its worship into the public space on a grand scale.

Windows into our World

In Parts 1 and 2 then, we offer some urban insights into worship that address the 'what' and the 'how to' questions. Finally, in Part 3, there are three contributions drawn from urban experience that invite a reconceptualization of liturgy and worship. In Chapter 7, Mark

Waters thinks about the meeting of three narratives in worship – those of the individual, the community and the Christian faith tradition. Erica Dunmow in Chapter 8 makes the case for the real world to be wrestled with in the sanctuary. My final contribution places worship in the daily and weekly pattern of our actions and decision-making.

Britain is currently a place where the value of faith communities in society is something that people are prepared to talk about once again. Worship is at the heart of our churches' lives. It is through worship that God is revealed, salvation history declared, God's people are formed and prayer offered. This can only happen in relation to the time and space we inhabit. I hope that through our working out of principle, experience and theory from the varied urban contexts we represent we can also bring some enrichment in perception of the urban church and its worship.

Tim Stratford
Kirkby

Part 1

WINDOWS INTO THE KINGDOM

1

Regeneration and the Kingdom of Heaven

JOHN AUSTIN

Not long ago I was part of a small group of people from the business world, statutory organizations, and faith and voluntary sectors in Birmingham, who had gathered to reflect on one of the policy initiatives of the Local Authority. The Council had decided to devolve many of its services to Ward level in order that the services could be more responsive to local needs. The idea was also part of an initiative to attempt to revive local democracy and included the plan to establish District or Constituency committees, giving people a local voice in how the services were to be managed. It is part of the Council's strategy for creating what it originally called 'Flourishing Neighbourhoods', though now the name has changed to 'Vital Urban Villages'.

What the group realized was that 'Flourishing Neighbourhoods' contained the germ of an idea that was much more than a trendy name for devolving Council services. Apart from this change in one significant area of the Council's responsibilities, almost no thought had been given to what a flourishing neighbourhood might look like. The group were very clear that neighbourhoods do not flourish simply as a result of devolution. Our consultant had asked us to select three words that would best characterize a flourishing neighbourhood. We found the first two characteristics easy to agree. A flourishing neighbourhood would first need to be one in which young and old alike felt safe both in their homes and in the streets. We also agreed that the neighbourhood needed to be clean. Its total physical environment should bear the hallmarks of being cared for, cherished and looked after, not simply free from litter and with its grass mown.

We had much more difficulty with the third characteristic. We tried a whole host of other characteristics such as 'economically vibrant', or 'child friendly', or 'efficient services', or 'good community facilities', but we sensed something was missing. It wasn't until the word 'generous' emerged that we felt we had hit upon an entirely different dimension which is crucial to our humanity and therefore crucial to creating communities in which human beings can flourish. Generosity touches on how neighbours look on each other. It speaks of respect and acceptance, and of welcome given to the diversities of people who live in any neighbourhood. It speaks of hospitality and welcome. In a city as diverse as Birmingham, that is so vital.

Reflecting later on this process I began to realize that although I had been involved in regeneration and community development for many years and had been chair of the Newtown/South Aston City Challenge Board which had the responsibility for a £37-million five-year programme, I had never had this kind of conversation before. It had always been assumed that people would flourish if they had better homes, reasonably secure jobs, had received training for the job market, where the resources going into the schools were such that the young people got more A*–C grades at GCSE, where derelict buildings were either pulled down, or renovated for community use. Of course, all these things are important and no community could flourish without them, but what that conversation with friends from the other sectors helped me to see more clearly was that the sort of things I had been involved with, which required us to measure, quantify and tick the relevant boxes for our funders to be certain that we were giving value for money, and meeting our targets, was missing an essential element. These things of themselves are not sufficient to ensure that communities will be ones in which people will truly flourish. I have never had a conversation, for example, with our City Challenge Board about the conditions in which human beings flourish. We were too busy trying to meet our targets and measuring the outcomes of the programme we had signed up for. With the wisdom of hindsight, we missed a crucially important discussion both as Board members and for the community itself.

What the conversation about generosity helped me to see is that you cannot talk about human flourishing or flourishing neighbourhoods without addressing the question of values. Values are essential to our humanity. People flourish in the context of trust, they wither in an environment of suspicion and neglect. They grow in an atmosphere of generosity but they harden in a culture of meanness. They blossom in a culture of affirmation and appreciation but shrivel in one of criticism and blame. Their humanity expands in practising compassion, but loses a sense of solidarity and fellow feeling if they are wrapped up in self-concern. They find freedom for themselves and others in forgiveness. Without it they remain imprisoned in their resentments, grudges or hatreds. (The initial period, after a neighbourhood or location has been awarded a considerable sum of money for regeneration purposes, is often the most difficult period as hidden resentments, jealousies and struggles for power are played out by vested interests of one kind or another. Discussion about the values that undergird human flourishing and that need to mark the processes of regeneration enables the various parties to begin to share a common vision and steer people away from what can become very destructive relationships and which often makes the beginning of a regeneration programme such a difficult time.)

We can probably all think of other values which are essential for human flourishing, but the point I want to make is that I have never been part of a conversation that has asked the question, 'What makes for human flourishing?' when discussing a particular programme or regeneration activity. I've never been part of a conversation that asks, 'How does such regeneration activity develop or nurture those values which all agree are fundamental to human flourishing?' They must therefore be fundamental to the regeneration of the communities we are concerned about. If we have no discussion about the values that are crucial to our humanity, is it any wonder so much of our regeneration does not produce the communities in which people grow and flourish, are energized and find fulfilment? If we do not have a debate about how these essential values are nourished, then there is a real danger that people will lose the language with which to articulate the one thing necessary. The language of values will atrophy and people can easily lose the capacity to name what it is they experience. So it is hugely important that Christians who are involved in regeneration initiatives stimulate the debate about what kind of values create communities in which human beings flourish.

We can take encouragement in all this for two fundamental reasons. The first is that values are natural to our humanity. They belong to our nature as human beings, they belong to the essence of our humanity as naturally as the air we breathe. And the second reason to take encouragement is that these human values belong to, and are inseparable from the Kingdom of Heaven. They are the values of the Kingdom and, as such, they speak about God with a directness and simplicity that neither preaches nor attempts to evangelize. It is precisely because they are natural, and belong to our humanity, that when we use this kind of language people know what we are saying and can understand what we are about, especially if we are living consciously by values we are seeking to commend.

It is vital to see that these values, so crucial for human flourishing, are inseparable from the Kingdom of God precisely because they are the values by which Jesus himself lived and through which he revealed the nature of his Father. They are the values that lead to life. We have to believe this passionately and stake our lives on them in the way he did. This is what it means to follow in the way of Jesus. It is the values of the Kingdom that we above all as Christians bring to the debate about regeneration and about what makes for human flourishing. Others will share those values and often shame us by the way they live them out, but without such commitment to the values of the Kingdom of Heaven, we have nothing distinctive to offer. Communities are transformed by the values they live by, and the quality of the relationships these values generate. Communities are not transformed by their affluence or by how much they possess, yet this is the assumption that lies behind almost all the regeneration programmes of recent years. Even those which are concerned with education are fundamentally about how we can equip youngsters or the unemployed with the skills which will help them enter the employment market and thereby cease to be what Zygmunt Bauman, in a memorable phrase, calls 'deficient consumers'.[1]

Yet this presents those of us involved in community projects and regeneration initiatives with a real challenge. How are we to witness to and articulate the values of the Kingdom in the complexities, messiness and pressures of our busy lives in the communities that we serve? The challenge is particularly sharp when we are working with partners who may have no faith at all, or who have a faith other than Christian, and whose only contact with the Church is likely to be through the projects we are involved in. How do we witness to the values of the Kingdom without being inappropriately evangelistic?

Ann Morisy, in her very thoughtful and helpful book *Beyond the Good Samaritan*, gives an excellent example.[2] She describes the way in which a local parish priest who chairs a local community project management committee always opens the meetings by suggesting the members spend a few moments of silence calling to mind why they are present. He reminds them that they are not there simply for their own benefit. They are not there to make a name for themselves. Everyone present shares a common goal which is to serve the well-being of their neighbours and to create the conditions in which ultimately everyone in the community can flourish. He sets the particular business of the meeting in a larger social context. From time to time he can refer back to it when they have to make difficult or contentious decisions. What he is doing helps all present to touch base with the deeper values which undergird their involvement.

Another marvellous example I heard of recently was of a parish priest who had spent over 15 years regenerating the plant of his church in an inner area of Birmingham which has a high proportion of Muslims living in the parish. He had begun not with the church but by establishing a café to be an unthreatening place for people within the locality to meet, and to be something of a focus of community which until then had not existed. Attached to it was a job centre, through which people were helped into employment. From there he created a nursery out of a dilapidated church hall. This not only provided nursery places for 30 children, many of whom came from the Muslim community, but employment for 18 full- and part-time staff and training placements for Muslim girls wanting a career in child care. Only then did he tackle the redevelopment of the church itself, which had remained an ugly barn of a place. This he turned into a highly flexible church and conference centre that is used by a whole variety of organizations including the Local Authority and training agencies. The whole developed complex now has 35 people, both full- and part-time on site, many of them Muslim and a considerable number without any religious affiliation at all. It has become a sizeable management task, which requires that from time to time they all meet in order to understand the situations facing each partner and strand within the overall project and how they can help one another.

At one of these periodic away days together the parish priest who headed the whole enterprise suggested they talk about forgiveness. He opened the day by asking the forgiveness of the whole team for the ways in which he had let them down through his inattention, busyness, or high-handed ways in which he had made decisions without consulting them. This had a remarkable effect. Tears were shed. Hard truths were faced. Many, particularly from the Muslim community, said it was unique in their experience for a person in authority to ask forgiveness of those 'beneath' him. This led to an extraordinary discussion of how forgiveness is crucial for our humanity because it has its roots in the forgiveness of God. It is a wonderful example of mission and evangelism arising out of a profound concern for the community and its needs and of the Church's commitment to creating the conditions in which people can flourish.

Yet the challenge to articulate the values of the Kingdom of Heaven lies not only in the contribution Christians have to make to regeneration. It is a challenge that faces congregations in their own life together. I mentioned earlier I had never been part of a conversation with partners in the field of regeneration about what made for communities in which people flourish. The truth is that I have never had that kind of a conversation with any church congregations either. It is now quite the fashion that congregations create for themselves Mission or Vision Statements in which they develop strategies through which they seek to implement their vision. These cover such areas as worship, lay development, youth work and the nurture of children, and the pastoral care of the bereaved and the housebound. But I have never had a conversation with a congregation about the values they wish to live by, through which they will witness to the Kingdom Jesus came to establish and which he bade his disciples seek above all else. The challenge for congregations is to be as clear as they can about the most important values they wish to enshrine in their common life together. Given their focus on Jesus as revealing the nature of the Father, the gift of the Spirit and their mission that men and women should have life in all its fullness, Christian congregations should be communities of human flourishing, where the values of the Kingdom are most in evidence.

The implications of all this for our worship are enormous. It means that everything we do in the way we worship needs to be tested for how it nurtures us in the values of the Kingdom: trust, generosity, affirmation, compassion and forgiveness. There also needs to be space in our worship for the anger, despair and grief of communities and people to be brought into the realm of God's generosity and forgiveness in order that they may be transformed into new confident and flourishing human beings. Do we have the faith and trust that what for us is impossible is nonetheless possible for God?

Reflecting the passion and pain of our communities means that our worship cannot be monochrome. At different seasons of the year different values will naturally find a focus in our worship. At Christmas, generosity, trust, simplicity, humility are some of the values that come to mind. In Lent, the values of compassion, solidarity with suffering humanity, sharing the goods of the earth, and care for the earth itself, valuing and not abusing the abundance of creation, could all be part of a passion for justice appropriate for the season of the year. Other seasons can be used to nurture us in other values that reflect our commitment to the Kingdom of Heaven.

However, while the content of our worship is of course very important, what is even more crucial is the way our worship is presented, the hymns and songs we sing (most of us learn our theology through what we sing rather than through what we listen to or read), and the themes we choose, the care given to the pew leaflet, and the way the altar is prepared, who reads the lessons and how they are read, the breadth and depth of the intercessions and how carefully they are prepared in order to be authentically the Prayers of the People. All are expressive of the values we bring to our worship. It is not only the words of our worship that matter but the details of its choreography, the spirit of its offering and the inclusive generosity it expresses and enlarges.

A good example of how one congregation has integrated its commitment to the values of the Kingdom of Heaven into its worship, is by its Liturgy Group carrying out a values audit of the various acts of worship their church holds during the week, not only for the principal Sunday services. They asked, 'In what ways does this particular act of worship nurture the life of God in the People of God for the Kingdom of God?' They looked at the details of each act of worship, from the way people were welcomed at the door, especially newcomers and strangers, to the way it enabled participation and celebrated the diverse gifts of its people, especially its children and young people. This recognized that all the values of the Kingdom can be expressed in every act of worship, which is why they looked at all the services including those for special occasions.

It is often said by those who do not go to church that you don't have to go to church to be a Christian, by which they mean you don't have to go to church to believe in God or to live a good, morally upright and sincere life. And of course that is true. However, if we are to avoid tempering our values and our commitments to our own convenience or to fit in too comfortably with the values and mores of our own group, class or tribe, then all of us need to articulate, to celebrate and to stand under the judgement of what we say we most believe in. For Christians, this is what we do Sunday by Sunday, especially in the celebration of the Eucharist, which is the most distinctively Christian activity Christians can do together. Worship is therefore *the* place in which to nurture the values of the Kingdom of Heaven and the place where Christians everywhere, in inner urban, outer estate, and more affluent suburb alike, are being transformed in themselves, and is a point of transformation within the communities in which they are set.

Notes

1 Zygmunt Bauman, *Work, Consumerism and the New Poor*, Buckingham: Open University Press, 1998, p. 38.
2 Ann Morisy, *Beyond the Good Samaritan*, London: Continuum, 1996.

2

'Singing the Lord's song'

KATHY GALLOWAY

This chapter was an address first given to the National Estate Churches Network Conference in 2004 and is reprinted here with permission of the author.

How shall we ever sing God's song, in such a foreign land?

'Singing the Lord's song in a strange land': the reference is to Psalm 137, that powerful and terrible lament of the Israelites in exile, and indeed, there are ways in which estate churches may resemble communities in exile, struggling to keep the rumour of God alive in the face of daunting social problems, exclusion, and often considerable poverty. In addition, you are struggling in the face of a culture which is largely indifferent to the Church, and whose indifference may be particularly marked in areas where the sheer business of survival is so demanding.

We live in a culture which is increasingly less dependent on the spoken or written word. Instead, it utilizes visual media extensively. People are not trained to listen for long to a speaker, nor to rely on oratory for stimulus, nor to depend upon books for knowledge. People do not nowadays commit a great deal of information to memory, nor learn things by rote or catechism. They merely need to know where data is stored and how to access it. Communication has undergone a paradigm shift, but the Churches have not, by and large, been part of it. We have entered the twenty-first century still wedded to nineteenth-century methods. It's salutary to remind ourselves, for example, that people remember approximately 80 per cent of what preachers say. They remember much more of how they say it. The medium is also the message! Every primary school teacher knows that people learn least from what they hear, a bit more from what they are shown, and most from what they take part in.

Cultural alienation from worship is quite acute. Recent research by the BBC discovered that the words 'church', 'service', 'Christian' and even 'God' in the title of a programme caused a large majority of people in every age group apart from the over-70s to switch off or change channels immediately. In the 16–24 age-group, every single one of them switched off.

Increasingly, people have little or nothing to do with the Church, and are completely unfamiliar with worship. Indeed, in housing estates, many people are 'unchurched' for several generations, have never been in a church, never opened a Bible or gained any accurate knowledge of Christianity. To people who know nothing about Christianity, the forms and language of Christian worship are not so much objectionable as incomprehensible or devoid of meaning. The idea of 'going to worship' is alienating, even threatening for many. To that extent, therefore, worship is a profoundly counter-cultural activity.

We are accustomed to thinking of this counter-cultural status as a problem, to seeing ourselves as either struggling to hold back the tide of indifference like King Canute, and with as little success, or as retreating into increasingly sectarian, defensive fortresses, ideologically driven and guarding our purity against a nasty secular world which is out to get us. However, I think there is another way of celebrating that counter-cultural status, of seeing it as an opportunity rather than a problem, in the context of housing estate churches.

A religious community which does not hunger and thirst for justice to be done bears false witness

Prophetic voices are those which read the signs of the times in the light of the justice and love of God, and speak out against all that distorts or diminishes the image of God in human beings. In doing so, they may come into conflict with the status quo, with powerful interests who have an investment in the way things are. They may struggle with questions of resisting and confronting established power. It is my belief that there are many people in Britain today who find themselves at the sharp end of the dominant power that is our economic system.

In the economic landscape of Britain, there are whole communities that are almost entirely redundant to the economy. They have little market value. They have no capital. Their labour is either redundant or low-waged. They have very little consumer clout because they don't have enough spending power to be attractive, except to the people who sell money, or, to give them their old name, moneylenders, and the drug dealers. Their environment does not value them to the point where their children may be suffering from malnutrition. Furthermore, these communities are most likely to be the ones which are symbolically undesirable and politically irrelevant. That is, they are a blot on the landscape, and most of them don't vote, or their votes are taken for granted. They aren't around, their voices aren't heard, people presume to speak for them when policy is made that shapes their lives and communities.

This scenario is one which relentlessly distorts or diminishes the image of God in human beings. It is also one in which people come into conflict with the status quo, with powerful interests who have an investment keeping things the way they are. They too may struggle, with questions of resisting and confronting established power. This is a hegemony, acutest of course in the poorest countries of the world, but equally present in pervasive ways in this country, as much as the one which faced the people of Israel. So I believe that singing the Lord's song in a strange land means first of all that Churches need to be prophetic voices, reading the signs of the times in the light of the justice and love of God, and speaking out against all that distorts or diminishes the image of God in human beings.

Of course, there are many ways in which we do this – through public witness, community action, political lobbying, creating the alternative local economics which challenge this power. But this also affects the ways we pray and sing and share word and sacrament.

The Old Testament scholar, Walter Brueggemann, reflecting on Israel as a community of intentional resistance to the oppressive power of Egypt, identifies what he calls *liturgical resistance*, the imagination of a free space outside the hegemony of the oppressor. Through the regular re-enactment of the Exodus story, using poetry, sacrament, sign and drama, it provides a script for an alternative practice, which incorporates:

- the public voicing of pain;
- a critique that ridicules established power;
- the song and dance of the women as a gesture of defiance.

I find this notion of liturgical resistance both helpful and inspirational here. To imagine a free space outside the hegemony of oppression, where people are no longer defined by their powerlessness, their low status, their invisibility, but instead by their valuation in the sight of God, to live for a little by God's economy rather than the markets, is, I think, an empowering thing. This alternative practice is truly counter-cultural, rather than just being the death throes of a dying institution.

What might this alternative practice look like?

The public voicing of pain

> How long, O Lord will you quite forget me?
> How long, O Lord will you turn your face from me?
> How long, O Lord must I suffer in my soul?
> How long, how long, O Lord?[1]

These words from Psalm 13 are a powerful reminder that we have resources for the public voicing of pain. After weeks of visiting British churches, an Argentinian asked, 'Where in your worship do you express your suffering?' 'Do you mean, where do we pray for the world or confess our sins?' was the reply. 'No,' he said, 'I mean, where in your worship can your people say, this hurts me, or, I am angry about this?' No one could answer him. We do not have the confidence of the black Churches where the leader will say openly, 'our brother, our sister is troubled', and will depart from the order of worship to listen to their story and speak words of consolation and encouragement. I almost said, stop the worship. Yet it's not stopping it; it's simply grounding it in the lived reality of the people.

And it's not just about words, it's about singing. People have for centuries sung their pain, and found that singing can express what the spoken word stumbles, or is trite about. The metrical Psalms of my Presbyterian tradition, the chanted or intoned Psalms of Catholic traditions have served that purpose for generations. I am not sure that these particular musical traditions really move people in the way they used to; my colleague John Bell has made wonderful arrangements of the Psalms to contemporary or folk tunes, and they have resonated deeply with many. This is the powerful attraction of gospel music, of spirituals, of the blues, of soul music. Pain needs music that can speak to, and of the soul.

I think that we are sometimes overly wordy and pompous about confessing our sin too. For people who know very well their own frailty, whose society never lets them forget it, this can become a kind of burden to lay on people's backs. Less sin and more grace might feel more like good news to the poor.

> Amazing grace, how sweet the sound that saved a wretch like me.
> I once was lost, but now am found, was blind, but now I see.[2]

And am seen. The Japanese theologian, Kosuke Koyama, has written:

> Grace cannot function in a world of invisibility. Yet in our world the rulers try to make invisible the alien, the orphan, the hungry and thirsty, the sick and imprisoned. This is violence. Their bodies must remain visible. There is a connection between invisibility and violence. People, because of the image of God they embody, must remain seen. Faith, hope and love are not vital except in what is seen. Religion seems to raise up the invisible and despise what is visible. But it is the 'see, hear, touch' gospel that can nurture the hope which is free from deception.[3]

There must be places where pain can be publicly voiced, one place where people's suffering is not tidied away. The things that move us and disgust us underneath the faces we show to the world are not the things we are comfortable with in church. What we do with our money; the embarrassing agonies of adolescence and the equally real agonies of facing a lonely old age; sexuality and the messy, endlessly fascinating business of relationships; difficulties at work or the confidence-shattering experience of redundancy; the weariness of single parenthood or the paralysing fear of failure, of dangerous streets and a dangerous world; all the pleasures and frailties of body and spirit: these are the places where we live on the knife-edge of faith.

If we cannot honestly bring them with us into worship, then our worship becomes sanitized, talking about everything except what is really important to us. Disconnected from our lives, it ceases to refresh, to matter. Ultimately, it dies. Finding the words and shapes to name and share our lives in liturgy is not easy. It is exposed. It means trying new things which often do not seem beautiful or dignified. It may be painful, inadequate, odd, faltering. But, then, so are our lives! And song has such an important part to play, because it allows people to express their pain publicly without violating their privacy.

A critique that ridicules established power

Don't tell me of a faith that fears
to face the world around
Don't dull my mind with easy thoughts
of grace without a ground
I need to know that God is real
I need to know that Christ can feel
The need to touch and love and heal
The world, including me.[4]

The critique that ridicules established power is mostly not an easy one for Churches to hear, although they are quite good at making it. One of the things that gives the great prophetic voices of the Old Testament such power is that they speak from and to all sections of society, calling the people of Israel to account for their crimes:

The oppression of the weak by the strong
The expropriation of peasants from their land
The eviction of smallholders
The enslavement of children.

Now we know very well that nearly three thousand years later, none of these crimes has disappeared from the face of the earth, and we rightly stand in judgement against them, condemn them, may be actively involved in campaigning against them. By the authority of Scripture, with the authorization of Church and tradition, we read the prophetic texts against a world which practises such things, and the world is found wanting.

At this point, it may be important to remember that the words of the prophets were actually addressed quite specifically to the community of faith, to the people of the covenant. The prophets of the Old Testament did not appear out of nowhere, their critique was not an external one; they stood within a prophetic tradition and it was because of their belonging within the community that they understood so well the nature of the faith of Israel. Their critique was historical, contextual, directed against specific concrete social and economic practices in a particular place at a particular time.

And it was precisely because they were people who had been liberated by the Exodus, had received both the Law and the promise, that the community of faith was particularly under judgement. Of all people, they were the ones who should turn from oppressing and enslaving others.

And, as followers of Jesus, sharers in the new covenant, we too have to take a relationship to the judgement of the world. By the authority of Scripture, church and tradition, we stand in judgement on the world and find it wanting, but that judgement is a two-edged sword. For in confronting the world with our texts and dogmas, we are in turn confronted by the world, which shows us to ourself as church.

So the critique of established power also includes the power of the Church:

> Don't tell me of a faith that fears
> to face the world around
> Don't dull my mind with easy thoughts
> of grace without a ground.[5]

There is something important about songs and liturgies which are concrete, specific, rooted in daily life; which use language which people can understand, which name names:

> Inspired by love and anger, disturbed by need and pain,
> Informed of God's own bias, we ask God once again
> 'How long must some folk suffer? How long can few folk mind?
> How long dare vain self-interest turn prayer and pity blind?'
>
> From those forever shackled to what their wealth can buy,
> The fear of lost advantage provokes the bitter cry:
> Don't query our position, don't criticise our wealth,
> Don't mention those exploited by politics and stealth.[6]

These are questions that need to be asked as much of the Church as of society.

These song words are taking seriously Paul's often overlooked words from 1 Corinthians 14.15–17:

> What should I do, then? I will pray with my spirit, but I will also pray with my mind. I will sing with my spirit, but I will sing also with my mind. When you give thanks to God in spirit only, how can an

ordinary person taking part in the meeting say Amen to your prayer of thanksgiving. He has no way of knowing what you are saying. Even if your prayer of thanks to God is quite good the other person is not helped at all.

Paul was talking about speaking in strange tongues, but a lot of religious and liturgical language is a pretty strange tongue.

A critique is not the same as a criticism. It's one of the ways we learn. From the critique of others, and our own self-critique, here are some of the things we think we have learned about singing the Lord's song:

- We speak of the gospel as holy; that is, it heals the splits and divisions within us and between us, between the material and the spiritual, the personal and the political. Therefore, our liturgy must also be integrative, must name both the tensions and the connections and offer them up to be transformed – not in abstract, but as they show up in the struggles of everyday life. A friend was a miner during the British miners' strike of the early 1980s. In this protracted and bitter conflict, which affected every home in the village, the minister did not once refer to any aspect of the strike in either preaching or prayer. The people of this community were left to struggle with almost unendurable realities bereft of any word of wholeness from this official representative of the gospel. The word of life that saved them was ministered to them in the soup kitchens and the homes of the mostly unchurched. No wonder my friend felt betrayed by the Church.
- And we believe that the gospel is participative. In the great drama of salvation, we are not merely spectators. Our metaphors are participative ones – but we don't make it easy for people to write themselves into the story. We depend on what we so often fulminate against in popular culture, the vicarious. It is perfectly possible to create structures for more corporate sharing. We rarely even allow sufficient silence and space in worship to allow people to reflect and engage inwardly in what should be a participative process.
- And we believe that the gospel is inclusive. Yet the reality we too often communicate through our arcane and inaccessible jargon and forms is that of insiders and outsiders. It is not a long step from here to 'the other' becoming 'the problem', and we ourselves

becoming sectarian. Sometimes the Church's projection of its own collective fear and disgust on to those who are 'not us' can revolt all that is humane and sensitive in people, and undermine the credibility of our professed truth.

- Because we believe that the gospel is redemptive. In the God who runs out to meet us is always the possibility of healing and transformation. In any good film, the redemptive possibility of truth, and the tensions which afflict people as they grope towards it, are vividly dramatized, and we, caught up in the drama, experience something of that redemption. In a culture in which visual media are so powerful, it may well be the case that more people experience the Word breaking in through Saturday night at the movies than on Sunday morning in church.

To seek this consistency of medium and message in our liturgy demands the courage to change, to discern what of our tradition is still vivid and appropriate, and what needs to be expressed in new ways. Otherwise, the demanding common task of loving our neighbour will become increasingly fragmented, a source of anxiety and division rather than of hope and liberation.

I want to say a little about worship as the *work of the people*. By this, I mean the considerable and regular involvement of the members of the church in the planning, preparation and leadership of worship. For our clerically dominated worship, this is a big shift; it requires hard work, a less dependent relationship between minister and people, and a willingness for clergy to take on a much more enabling role. This kind of participation is far more appropriate to the society we actually live in rather than that role being modelled on a society we used to live in.

If, Sunday by Sunday, you are asked to pray, then you are faced with questions. What need today is pressing, what lack of faithfulness, where in the world is the hurt and injustice that moves us? You have to select, to discern meaning and significance. If you are asked to reflect on your life in the light of the gospel, then you will eventually come face to face with two questions: 'Who do people say that I am?' and 'Who do you say that I am?'

Jesus was always asking questions . . . God or Caesar? . . . do you want to be healed? . . . who, then, loved him more? . . . do you love me? This dialectical process is the way we grow to maturity from childhood. Should the Church, in our attachment to giving answers, be the only place which should not encourage this most proven spiritual formation?

The fact that this involves people with no formal theological training is often cited as a factor against participation. On the contrary, a lack of defensive manoeuvres means that theirs is often among the most exposed and therefore most honest contribution; in that unguarded ground, they are wrestling with angels, limping away wounded, but with a name and a blessing. The ability to theorize and speculate can sometimes be a way of escaping engagement. George MacLeod said:

> There are times when our prayer life is refreshing: but analysed, they turn out to be the times when the pressures have been so weighty that you have simply had to go with them to God. But this is precisely the recovery of the knife-edge. The religious moment flows from the practical. When we have wrestled with our state and given it to God, the illuminative becomes our urgent need and not our pious obligation. In such a mood, the Bible is not something that 'ought' to be read, but its opening becomes a sheer necessity of our condition.[7]

There are a lot of people who, when asked what your value is, cannot retreat into theories of the atonement, but struggle with the question in a way that is neither simple nor unthinking precisely because their society treats them as practically valueless.

Martin Luther said, 'A man does not become a theologian by reading and knowing and understanding, but by living and dying and being damned.' This is the praxis of liberation theology.

The song and dance of the women as a gesture of defiance

I shall praise you, O God, from my soul
I shall praise you, O God, from my soul
Though my song be at odds with the will of earthly gods
I shall praise you, O God from my soul.[8]

For above all, the song and dance which is a gesture of defiance is so because it expresses hope and liberation. I met a woman once whose life had been completely turned around from being an alcoholic in an abusive marriage. She had been a Christian before, but had started to attend a Pentecostal meeting. I asked her what had made the change happen. She said, 'My priest could only offer me the cross – to go on enduring suffering. But the Pentecostal meeting gave me the hope of resurrection. It gave me back my life.'

Remember that Brueggemann describes the regular re-enactment of the Exodus story as providing a script for an alternative practice using poetry, sacrament, sign and drama. Christian worship too, has, over the centuries, evolved the way it has because it is the way *life* is, it is true to experience. It is the great drama of salvation, played in a different key.

It begins with gathering together in Christ's name, and the invitation to worship, and moves into the first act, the lost son act, of turning and heading for home. It is the act of still being a long way off.

In the heart of the second act is God's response to our distress: 'But while he was still far off, his father saw him and was filled with compassion; he ran and put his arms round him and kissed him.' The Word is the word of life, it is the good news of God running out to meet us while we are still far off.

And the third act dramatizes our response to God. The father tells us what to do. It is to celebrate with a feast. It is thanksgiving: 'for he was dead but now he is alive'. It is intercession and ministry to others: 'bring out the best robe quickly, put it on him, and a ring on his finger and shoes on his feet'. It is the gratitude of the profligate younger brother in us and the disciplining of the holier than thou elder brother in us. It is the reconciliation of brother to brother. 'You are always here with me, and everything I have is yours. But we have to celebrate and be happy because he was lost and now he is found.' And, finally, we are blessed, and sent back out with a task to do and good news to proclaim.

It is of the essence of Christianity that it is historical; it does not apply to some abstract or spiritual realm outside the temporal. Reality does not allow us to escape from history. In worship, we restore to memory and hope the broken body of Christ, in whose wounds are named all the violence of the world.

From Koyama again:

> Is hope related to the future? Yes. But even more, it is related to love. Hope is not a time-story. It is a love-story. The gospel dares to place

love above time. All the healing stories of the gospels, and ultimately the confession of the faith that 'on the third day he rose again
from the dead' point to this awesome truth. Hope is as impassioned
by love as is every healing word and action of Jesus.[9]

Koyama thinks hope is a hot love story. That's something to sing about,
isn't it? Something to dance about? And not just for women. When
people's lives are bleak in so many respects, when they feel powerless and despairing, the most truly counter-cultural thing people can
do is live, even for a little while, joy and hopefulness. Pentecostal
Churches know that. This is not escapism. It is liturgical resistance,
but it needs to be of the body and mind as well as of the spirit.

When John Bell says, 'Everyone can sing', I don't think he means
that everyone can or should sing badly. I don't want to put words in
his mouth, but I understand him as saying that first of all, everyone
has the potential to enjoy singing, because it's an enjoyable thing to
do, to lift your heart and your voice and express something in song.
The activity of singing has intrinsic value regardless of one's degree
of competence in it. Till recently, I suppose I would have made an
exception and said, anyone can sing, unless they're deaf or dumb. But
then a couple of months ago, I was at a meeting where a young deaf
woman signed a song, and communicated such pleasure in doing so,
that I realized that I was wrong about that too – she had her own
voice and her own language, and she sang with her heart and her hands.

For some people, however, the capacity to enjoy singing has been
denied them, because someone has told them that they couldn't
sing, so they shouldn't sing, so they don't sing. Now I happen to think
that the enjoyment of singing is a God-given gift, and therefore a human
right, and to tell someone they can't sing, or paint, or write poetry,
or whatever, is a seriously hurtful thing to do. So I really appreciate
what my Wild Goose colleagues have done over the years to release
that potential for people.[10] And I think what they've done is what all
good teachers do.

Knowing that no one likes to make a mess of things, and that one's
enjoyment of anything is enhanced by at least a basic grasp of the
essentials, they've developed ways to help people do it better. They've
started off by demystifying the process, showing that it's perfectly
possible to sing tunefully and joyfully without being able to read
music and without needing to have instrumental accompaniment, just

by trusting the capacity of the ear to listen and the mind to learn. They've found helpful ways to teach songs . . . and new and lively songs to sing.

Because they work mostly with people who are not trained singers, they've also emphasized the fact that you don't need to be in a choir, or a band, or to be a solo singer to enjoy singing and do it well. A good choir is a lovely thing, but it's certainly not the only place where good singing is found. And it can lay unhelpful expectations on singers. Something doesn't have to be difficult or complicated to be good. When it's assumed that people will sing, they will; when it's inferred that 'they might not manage it', they usually don't.

Helpful methods of sharing skills are empowering for people, and so is having a context to sing in. Singing for worship is one of them, of course, but so is singing in the context of political protest or actions, or as a demonstration of solidarity with the struggles of people; as the expression of deep sorrow or love or as a means of building community, or as a way of making unpleasant or routine tasks into something much more enjoyable. Having a good reason to sing is a great way of shifting the emphasis away from the singers and on to the song. And the ability to lose oneself in the song is the best way of getting over the performance anxiety that's at the root of so many of our fears and reluctance to take the risk of doing the new thing, even if we secretly want to do it.

And most of all, good teachers are encouraging, and go on being encouraging. They let you try things and fail at them, but they encourage you to try again and again. There's a wonderful painting in the National Portrait Gallery of a scene from Samuel Beckett's *Waiting for Godot*. The caption on it reads, 'No matter. Try again. Fail again. Fail better.' The best teachers are the ones who encourage you to be the best that you can be, give you the confidence that that's better than you thought, but don't lay the burden of perfection on you. You don't have to sing like Pavarotti or Marvin Gaye or Alicia Keys, or whoever your particular icon of perfection is. You can sing in your own voice, and, as they say about parenting, you can be good enough! Hey, maybe the problem all along was not that you couldn't sing, but that the teacher couldn't teach. Maybe you are the best teachers after all.

God asks, 'Who will go for me?
Who will extend my reach?

And who, when few will listen,
will prophesy and preach?
And who, when few bid welcome,
will offer all they know?
And who, when few dare follow,
will walk the road I show?'[11]

Notes

1 John L. Bell and Graham Maule, from *Heaven Shall Not Wait*, Glasgow: Wild Goose Publications, 1987.
2 'Amazing Grace', John Newton.
3 Kosuke Koyama, from an address given at the WCC General Assembly, Harare, 1998.
4 Bell and Maule, *Enemy of Apathy*, Glasgow: Wild Goose Publications, 1988.
5 Bell and Maule, *Enemy of Apathy*.
6 Bell and Maule, *Heaven Shall Not Wait*.
7 George MacLeod, *Only One Way Left*, Glasgow: Iona Community, 1956.
8 Bell and Maule, *Love and Anger*, Glasgow: Wild Goose Publications, 1997.
9 Koyama, address.
10 The Wild Goose Resource Group is a semi-autonomous project of the Iona Community. It exists to support and equip congregations and clergy in the shaping and creation of new forms of relevant participative worship and adult learning.
11 Bell and Maule, *Heaven Shall Not Wait*.

3

Liturgy as the people's work

JOHN VINCENT

If worship is to be a window for the lives of Christian urban people, the worship must take its nature and character from those lives. The word 'liturgy' comes from the Greek word *leiturgia*, which literally means the work or service offered by someone, initially to the state, but then in acts of religious worship. The notion of work or service is prominent in early usage of the term. Liturgy is the work, the *ergon*, of the laity, the *laos*.[1]

What the Church has made of liturgy is something else. Liturgy has become set forms, led by appointed persons, rather than an offering of a community of people. Eucharist becomes a fixed, priest-led ritual, rather than a shared meal of disciples sharing a common privilege. Offices become set forms led by an appointed leader, rather than a common reading and prayer based on Scripture and experience.

But it could be different. And maybe the urban scene – where paid leaders, professionals, and even literate people are not very numerous – can be a place for liturgy's popular recovery.

It is perhaps worth reflecting, as an aside, on the consequences of the Eucharist or Lord's Supper being removed from the spheres of 'the people's work'. In denominations where services other than those involving the sacrament are regularly available, those services acquire a significantly alternative 'feel' and rationale. The lay reader in the Anglican Church conducts one in every two services; the Methodist local preacher conducts four out of every five services. The Baptists and the Free Churches experience a service of word, sermon, intercession and praise, which is the regular Sunday worship, with a sacrament of the Lord's Supper usually monthly.[2] Methodists typically have a 'sacrament of Holy Communion' monthly or, in smaller chapels, quarterly.[3] As Anglican ordained personnel become less

25

numerous, the number of lay-led or non-sacramental services increases, especially in rural areas.[4]

This concentration of sacramental worship to the ordained has two obvious consequences. The ordained become more and more sacramental priests or presidents, whose ministry naturally becomes concentrated on doing everything within, alongside, before or after the 'essential bit', so that their liturgical innovations or additions are either non-existent or are mainly sacrament-related. Meanwhile, the non-ordained develop a non-eucharistic spirituality and liturgical practice, which functions more or less independently of the Eucharist-centred spirituality and liturgical practice of the Eucharist-dependent clergy or Eucharist-dominant worship occasions.[5]

Particularly in the Free Churches, this has been the scene for a riotous development and flowering of experimental, participative, responsorial and often 'one-off' forms of worship, which demand a ready-made and constantly changing reservoir of written material.[6] This material is used in many non-eucharistic evening services in mainline churches and congregations, and increasingly in Anglican churches and cathedrals. Taizé worship, Iona worship, meditation, experimental and silent worship are the most obvious forms of this.

Yet using written forms of other creative writers or religious communities is not in itself 'liturgy as the people's work'. The liturgies written down might have begun as 'the people's work', but once written down and used by others they become 'liturgy of other people's work'. This is a particularly regrettable development in denominations in which extempore prayer has been the custom. It is generally recognized that the 'extempore' prayer of the preacher or worship leader can easily become almost as stereotyped as the written liturgies of congregations which all 'read from the same book'. Yet the extempore prayer in its classic form was a (less or more prepared) spontaneous utterance, however much it contained scriptural or liturgical phrases and ideas. The constant production of new 'pieces of paper' introduced by preachers and worship leaders is often counter-productive. Congregations are assumed to be willing to use forms of words only just invented by the liturgist, without preparation, much less agreement, by the congregation. Again, this is not 'liturgy as the people's work'.

Of course, it may be argued that 'the people' do not want to 'work' at creating liturgy. In Methodism, we have in the past decade regularized a new order of 'worship leaders', who conduct or lead worship in their own or in other churches. Such people invariably use considerable imagination and creativity in crafting appro-priate forms of worship, and naturally are grateful for the increasing volume of material available for their preparation, whether or not they end up in prepared and photocopied 'orders of worship' or 'responsive prayers' which are distributed to the worshippers. Often, 'worship groups' do the preparation, which certainly involves some 'work' by several members together.

'Liturgy as the people's work', then, is liturgy done by ordinary Christians, lay people. Historically, liturgy by groups of lay people was the foundation of the synagogue-type worship of the earliest Christians. The earliest shared meals were clearly 'real meals', and their separation from 'the Lord's Supper' is advised in only one local sit-uation by Paul, in 1 Corinthians 11.17–34. It is hard to know whether this advice was known elsewhere, or whether normally the early Christians 'shared their meals together with sincerity and joy' (Acts 2.46), as the most appropriate way of continuing the meals of Jesus with his disciples.[7] Certainly, the description of the gathering of Christians in 1 Corinthians 14.26 contains no reference to a 'Lord's Supper' element. 'When you come together,' it says, 'each one brings a Psalm, or a Scripture, or a revelation, or a tongue-speaking, or an interpretation of tongues.' Tongue-speaking must only take place when there is an interpreter (v.27), but two or three prophets may speak, and the rest weigh what they say (v.29). 'You can all prophesy one by one, so that all may learn and be encouraged' (v.31). The prime interest of Paul is that, whatever happens 'be for people's up-building' (v.26).[8]

Beyond this, it may be recalled that the 'daily offices' of the monastic orders were and are mainly built upon the Psalms, other Scriptures and non-eucharistic prayers, as indeed are the spiritual writings of the Middle Ages. The Reformers in the sixteenth cen-tury, while regarding the Lord's Supper as important, yet de-veloped non-eucharistic patterns of worship which became the norm in Protestantism. In recent decades, the progressive disappear-ance of non-eucharistic worship in Anglicanism has led some at least to regret the demise of Scripture- or exposition-centred worship.

All this does raise the question as to how far eucharistic worship was intended as the norm for Christian gatherings – a debate probably worth having, if it is possible to have such debates in the present 'ecumenical consensus' about the sacraments.[9] The story needs to be rediscovered of how 'Do this as a continuation of myself' came to be applied to the Last Supper only, over against the more difficult and demanding commands of Christ elsewhere in the gospels – or indeed in the practice of the earliest Christian communities. That is too large a question for us here; but it is significant how in situations where the Eucharist becomes too staid a part of the traditional practices of churches, non-eucharistic worship springs up to supplement or even supplant it.

Some 'people's liturgies'

Every instance of a 'people's liturgy' arises from a single Christian community. In the cases I will use, they all share certain characteristics.

First, they arise within small communities. The number of people who can realistically work together in liturgical creation is invariably limited. Where a liturgy is used in a large congregation but prepared by a small group, proper negotiation may take some time. In some congregations, the legitimacy of smaller, self-appointing, culturally distinctive and internally coherent groupings using the creative elements for new liturgies is recognized. In that case, the group functions as a mini-congregation itself. Probably more frequently, and certainly regularly in the instances which follow, the creative group are themselves a congregation of one or two dozen members only.

Second, the creative congregational members share the same context, and are often engaged in the same mission or project. They are creating forms which make sense to them in their context, and reflect their understandings and their experiences of attempting discipleship in those contexts. The liturgies are 'indigenous', deriving from the internal dynamics of particular disciple groups. They claim to be authentic to the place, the people, and the project of their context. They are 'local' liturgies.[10]

Third, the liturgies are performed or experimented with, and probably discussed (sometimes endlessly!) within the worshipping group, so that there is a continuing process of trial and error. The liturgy is not the creation of one person, who sits at her/his computer composing pieces for the next occasion. Rather, the liturgy

evolves experimentally, gaining from the contributions or participation and critique of all the members. Each member's gifts are
honoured. Often, drafts are used over a period of time, so that members have the opportunity for reflection and review, and proposing
alternatives.

Fourth, the liturgies are seen as supportive of mission and vocation. The groups do not see worship as an end in itself, but rather as
the support for members' ministries and wider local neighbourhood
concerns. The liturgy is not the first thing: the Christian 'movement',
the appearing of signs of the Kingdom of God, is the first thing. The
liturgy is needed as a place to sink back into, away from the real presence of God in the secular and in the congregation and neighbourhood political and healing practice. The liturgy is not the driving force,
but the underground discipline and structure for the community's
vocation and mission.

Fifth, the liturgies all arise from interdenominational or postdenominational Christian communities. Specifically, the Grimesthorpe Methodist Church of ten members includes Anglican and
Church of Scotland members; the Burngreave Ashram has Roman
Catholic, Anglican, Evangelical and Methodist members and six
members without denominational membership; while the Ashram
Community consists of 45 members who are a mix of all the preced-
ing, plus Quakers, Baptists and post-church people.

The three examples of contemporary people's liturgies all share
these features. They each come from small Christian communities; each is originally highly context-specific; each was crafted
experimentally by the congregation itself; each sees worship as a
support for 'the movement' of God's Realm, support for the service
of Christ, rather than the service of Christ itself; and they each have
ecumenical or postdenominational Christian communities as their
origins.

This may seem to some readers highly eccentric, and even irrelevant, but these five factors might be the key to the churches of the
future. The majority of people in Britain today are outside our
churches, either because they were never in them, or because they have
left them.[11] It could be that the future strategy of Christianity in Britain
will be to develop precisely such apparently idiosyncratic, highly
specific, Christian communities. Some people in Britain today who
do not belong to churches might be interested in being involved in

small neighbourhood or other communities, that have their presence and ministry in specific contexts, that use people's interests and gifts, that put mission and local concerns first, and that do not demand the church membership disciplines of existing denominations.

Grimesthorpe Methodist Church

In 1980, the 12 surviving members of Wesley Hall, the 1927 Wesleyan 'Mission Hall' in the steelworks valley of Grimesthorpe, decided to sell their 500-seat property and move into two corner-shops. They were and are a member-congregation of the Sheffield Inner City Ecumenical Mission (SICEM).[12] Mission policy was to abandon where possible nineteenth-century stone church buildings – not to move out of the neighbourhoods and 'unite' with the nearest suburban church, but rather to move back into the area in more appropriate premises. SICEM policy has resulted in abandoning or demolishing traditional church buildings to create an interesting variety of 'plant' and presence: a newly created housing complex (Pitsmoor, 1973), a former off-licence and shop with flat (Grimesthorpe, 1980), a former public house (The Furnival, 1996), and a mix of shops, dance studio, flats and workshops (Burngreave Ashram, 2000).

Worship at 10.30 on Sunday mornings at Grimesthorpe takes place either in the smaller shop, with room for 16 people, or in the larger corner shop, with room for 40. Usually, the congregation numbers between 6 and 12, plus a few children.[13] After the first hymn or song, and a prayer, both geared to the kids, we share what the children will do. One of them takes the collection, and they leave. The Bible readings follow, always read around the room, a verse each. People delight to have their turn, often struggling with their eyesight or with difficult words. If something strikes someone in the reading, they easily comment on it.

After more singing, we are at prayer in intercession. In this, we talk together about whatever is concerning us, with names of absent members, or sick friends, neighbours or relatives. The group especially bears a real sense of burden for the troubles of the world. We might talk together for at least 10 minutes in anguish about Kosovo, or the bombing of Iraq. Then the preacher closes with a prayer of two or three sentences, and we say the Lord's Prayer. The topics people have named do not need to be forced into a final prayer.

Our sharing has been the prayer, our caring has been the offering to God.

Then comes the sermon, which almost always opens out into conversation and reflection. No one is too shy to have their say. Visiting preachers are advised to make their initial points important, in case the congregation picks up on them, and they never reach their later points!

After the last singing, the children burst in again and dance around showing us what they have been doing. Or we all have to go into the big room to see their efforts on the walls. A child is allowed a few minutes on the piano, learning some hymn tune with one finger. Tea, juice and biscuits appear for all, and we move around chatting, reluctant to break it up and go home.

The Grimesthorpe Sunday morning liturgy is certainly 'the people's work'. Usually, no written forms are used, except for the hymn books (*Methodist Hymn Book*, *Hymns and Psalms*, and *New Orbit* [Galliard]), plus song sheets of mainly contemporary children's songs. Communion occasions use booklets from the 1976 *Methodist Service Book*. Visiting preachers and local worshippers occasionally bring other pieces of written material, but not usually for unison use. The liturgy is seen as composed spontaneously from the stories and insights of the worshippers, with strong emphasis on local community concerns and issues, neighbourhood politics, service provision, and the personal lives of the membership and the wider Christian community. These liturgies are always extempore, and never recorded or written down.

Grace Vincent's description of the Grimesthorpe worship concludes:

> It seems to me that there are three significant and essential characteristics of this kind of worship. First, the room and the numbers are both small. In what larger churches would old or shy and inarticulate people feel free to contribute? Because we know each other well, there is no artificial, formal talk. Conversation is real and about real things, and rarely in 'religious' language. Secondly, there is a basic assumption that we are all in this together, that everyone is valued and takes responsibility for what happens. So their thoughts are heard. It is a corporate ministry of all the members. Thirdly, the understanding is that we are there for each other, for the children, for the local community, and for the whole world. The context is tiny, but the brief is vast.[14]

Burngreave Ashram

Burngreave Ashram, also a member of the Sheffield Inner City Ecumenical Mission, is a complex of buildings at 80 and 86 Spital Hill, in the centre of Sheffield's north-east inner city. Surrounded by ethnic shops, advice centres, foodstores and religious outlets, it functions from four separate but related areas: the corner shop, which houses a New Roots vegan/vegetarian/wholefoods shop and café, run by volunteers, several of whom are Burngreave Ashram members; the cellar space, for meetings, quiet room, weekly midday meditation ('all spiritualities welcome'), children's art occasions, a Saturday computer café ('your computers mended free'), and WEA and LEA classes; the studio, hired for parties and meetings, used for occasional SICEM and other worship occasions, and rented weekly by Kutumba African Dance and Music Group, and daily by Starting Point, a therapy service for post-drug users; and the first floor of 80, which is the One World Healing Centre. There are also two self-contained flats for people working in the project, soon to be added to by two further self-contained one-person flats, one for a part-time Warden.

The gathering takes place on Monday evenings in the homes of the members. There is a bring and share meal at 7 p.m., for which the host prepares a main dish. Conversation over the meal is usually about members' lives, work and interests, and about current local or national concerns. At 8 p.m., one of the members leads worship, liturgy, readings, prayers or meditation, sometimes from the Ashram Community Worship Book.[15] Then at 8.30 or so, another member introduces a theme, or a Bible study, or a part of an agreed series of studies.

One series has been what individual members really make of traditional doctrines like God, Christ, the cross, eternal life, suffering, the Kingdom of God, vocation, forgiveness, etc. Another series invited members to discuss and then write down their own personal beliefs, which are now bound together in a folder. Currently, we have a series by three members who at various stages did the Urban Theology Unit Study Year on Personal Theology and Mission. And we are finally getting around to what Ashram has got others doing up and down the country – running a *Journey* programme for enquirers and fellow-travellers, 'but chiefly ourselves'![16]

Burngreave Ashram describes itself, among other things in its Mission Statement, in these terms: 'As an Ashram, a place for personal and group spirituality, open to people of all religions and none, with its base in the radical Christian tradition, which expresses itself in the Gathering.' This means that we sometimes need to question whether an activity is intended to be specifically Christian, or mainly Christian catering also for others present, or intentionally multifaith. The number of the latter activities could grow, as Burngreave has 27 faith groups (12 Christian, 7 Muslim, plus most other faiths). We are core members of Burngreave Faiths in Community, and there is much that could be done in this area were there individuals prepared to do the necessary 'leg-work' over a few years.

Meantime, the Gathering has an ongoing project to write liturgies, which will doubtless eventually become part of the next edition of Ashram's *Community Worship*. The liturgies vary in the degree to which they are intentionally multifaith – most are specifically Christian. One attempt to write a multifaith liturgy for a small group of friends follows. It invites each person present to go through a liturgical process in their own consciousness, and to share with others as they do so, if and as they wish:

A Corporate Meditation for All Faiths and None
(*spoken together*)

We've come out of the world to be together in this place.
We bring our complicated and uncertain lives.
Can we share anything we are feeling at this moment?
(*People say a few brief words*)

We are here with our common humanity:
our fears (*pause for reflection*)
our frailty (*pause for reflection*)
our vulnerability (*pause for reflection*)
our mistakes (*pause for reflection*)
our regrets (*pause for reflection*)
our confusion (*pause for reflection*)

We are people who are aware of the world and its needs.
Can we share something of the needs of the world, both local or
    global?
(*People say a few brief words about needs in the world*)

We are also people with inner strengths and convictions.
We share the sources of our inspiration:
people
ideas
words
pictures
places
things
(*People say or think about their sources of inspiration*)

We commit ourselves to hold to the truth as we see it.

We share our current callings, commitments and intentions.
(*People speak of their present and planned practice*)

We commit ourselves to mutual support.
(*People hold hands in a circle and say together . . .*)

We support each other in preparedness to take action, to change
and to grow

There is, of course, in such a meditation, a strong opportunity for Christians actually to state their Christ- or Kingdom- or discipleship-related attitudes, prayers or commitments. The framework above obviously owes something to Christian worship experience but it means that Christians have to learn to be specific in their Christian convictions and beliefs by having to state them in a non-specifically Christian context. This is actually quite demanding, and many 'liberal' Christians are not well equipped for it! Equally, those who have only encountered or memorized beliefs in written liturgical forms have few easily accessible resources within, to contribute in such open situations.

Ashram Community

The Ashram Community Trust was formed in 1967, 'for Christian life and action in the world'. Its origins lie in the ecumenical communitarian movement of the 1960s, and led to five inner city community houses in the 1970s and 1980s, plus a wider community of members and associate members, presently around 50 and 40 respectively.

The Community's life consists of the separate, mutually supported vocations of each of its members, plus monthly or bi-monthly Branch half-days in various parts of the country, plus bi-annual residential

weekends, bi-annual day General Meetings, occasional visits and
retreats, and an annual holiday. Most members remain active and
committed in denominational local churches, Ashram being what
Mark Gibbs used to call their 'second church membership'. The six
areas of the Ashram Community Commitment (see below) indicate
the specific areas of the community's vocation.[17]

The worship life of the Community takes place in members' homes,
or at General or Branch meetings or at the weekends. Distinctive
Eucharist and agape services have been developed, plus Morning and
Evening Prayers, Housewarmings, and Commitments.[18] One of the
most original and characteristic services is the annual Commitment
Service, which takes place at the May Weekend, when those who have
joined for the new April–March membership year as full members
welcome each other into their common membership.

This particular annual liturgy is, to me, always a deeply moving
occasion, similar to the annual Methodist Covenant Service. Its particular value is that it provides not words for people to use (except
for the Commitment), but rather spaces in which each person provides their own words.

The liturgy proceeds as follows:

Membership Commitment Liturgy
The Membership Secretary leads the Community

All are welcome to participate as we come to the time of commitment. However, only those who have joined the Community for the
coming year, and whose membership card is now placed on the
central table, will be making their personal commitment formally and
publicly today.

Let us remember those who have walked before us in this commitment.
(*Past members may be named aloud by anyone*)

Let us remember those who share our commitment but are not with
us today.
(*Names of absent members are read out by Membership Secretary*)

We recognise with joy each person sharing their commitment with
the Community for the first time.
(*Names of new members are read out; they may also stand, introduce
themselves, or be introduced by an existing member*)

The commitment of Ashram Community members is:

> to hold to the Truth as it is in Jesus
> to support each other in good and ill
> to challenge evil with the power of love
> to offer the Kingdom in political and economic witness
> to work for the new community of all creation
> and to risk ourselves in a lifestyle of sharing.

Six areas of the space are labelled with these statements

Let us explore our commitment together.

Each moves to an area of commitment of their choice, and shares briefly with one or more members about how they plan to carry it out.

As each person is ready, those becoming members for the year ahead stand facing the centre. The others sit down. When there is silence, those standing say together:

I commit myself

> to hold to the Truth as it is in Jesus
> to support the others in good and ill
> to challenge evil with the power of love
> to offer the Kingdom in political and economic witness
> to work for the new community of all creation
> and to risk myself in a lifestyle of sharing.

Those standing go to the central table, take any membership card, and give it to its owner, greeting them with the words:

I honour your commitment, and seek to support you in it.
(*or any words they wish*)

All return to their places.
It may be appropriate to continue with a song in which all can join.

Conclusion

What do these experiences of worship suggest for the future? First, that we recognize the validity of pluralistic and extra-denominational forms of church. If the present policy of the main-line denominations continues, there will be fewer traditional church building- and church programme-style Christian communities. Those that survive will be needed to cover larger and larger areas or parishes. The

continuing more limited number of clergy of whatever denomination will be needed to care for such buildings, worship and
memberships, while also continuing to provide plant and services
for immediately post-church people requiring Christian baptisms,
weddings and funerals.

Alongside these, we will doubtless continue to see a growth of
house, shop-front and community congregations, with or without
connections to the main-line denominations. In this situation, the
model of the Ecumenical Mission needs to be developed, to provide connection and mutual support. SICEM, interestingly, in 2005
moved from shared financing of ministry in main-line denominations to a voluntary mutual support model involving other local
congregations.

Second, that we recognize that the present ordained clergy-
dependent model of church and worship is limiting the development
of contextual, indigenous church and worship. It is sometimes
stated that other groups cannot be relied upon to maintain Christian
orthodoxy. However, most main-line churches recognize how much
their own versions of the faith are dependent on historical develop-
ments which have landed them far removed from basic Christianity.[19]
Inasmuch as the main-line churches are catering for a diminishing
number of people, it becomes a strategy of vital importance that all
Christians, within and outside (or half-way of either!) those churches,
are given confidence and tools to work to develop with anyone who
would like to do so, a growing variety of para-denominational, postdenominational and interdenominational Christian congregations
and communities.[20]

Third, that we welcome a flowering in our time of many different Christian modes of congregational, liturgical and spiritual expression. The much condemned but growing 'smorgasbord' of alternative
spiritualities has come to stay, and we need to ensure that there are
a variety of Christian offerings available, alongside all the others.
We must not allow ourselves, or Christian faith, to be boxed into a
corner where we only have main-line denomination versions, probably increasingly 'coming together' to form even less diverse versions
of Christianity, in consequence of our understanding of 'unity'.

Fourth, that we recognize the need for an ever-expanding growth
of vernacular liturgies in a variety of different contexts. This growth
can be prevented by denominational activity. It can also be facilitated

by it. Urban churches especially can be expected to lead the way, as *The Cities* report recommended:

> City churches are providing Christians everywhere with opportunities for new forms of devotion and prayer, worship, hymnody and meditation. Churches should encourage, and provide support for, such expressions of indigenous and rooted spirituality from and for the city.[21]

Five practical conclusions which arise from all this can be stated:

1 It takes a long time for people to get round to creating indigenous liturgy if they have been in 'liturgical' churches. The development of urbane, vernacular, popular speech into forms which could be used by a group, let alone by a wider constituency, is not easy.

2 The orthodoxy of liturgy and prayer from popular groups depends upon its faithfulness to the practice of discipleship in that group, i.e. its orthopraxy, its faithfulness to the movement of the Realm of God on earth. Liturgy needs to be rewritten constantly in the light of the faithful practice of disciples in each place. Liturgy is serviced by practice, which is the defining mode of faith-life.

3 The development of liturgy as the people's work is best assisted, as in the three liturgies above, by congregations and facilitators working out, within different situations and for different purposes, appropriate *structures* and *'bare bones'*, which invite and facilitate people's own liturgical and spiritual creativity.[22]

4 Local liturgies should be allowed and encouraged to develop. Perhaps occasionally, outside facilitators could assist local worship leaders with the *expectation* and *methodology* of indigenous liturgy creativity, indicating how they might work from and develop their discipleship practice, biblical imagination, and theological discernment, into the direction of liturgical creativity.

5 Providers of liturgical forms might also assist the development of contextual indigenous liturgical expressions by making available a variety of short 'sample' forms (e.g. bidding prayers, thanksgiving frameworks, 'arrow' prayers, eucharistic liturgical elements such as epiclesis, words of institution, etc.). Similarly, such sample forms should be picked up from the contextual indigenous liturgical communities, as they are produced.

Notes

1 'Liturgy as the People's Work' derives from the original meaning of the word 'liturgy', as being the work – *ergon* – of the people – *laos*. Liturgy in this understanding is the creative work of a community of people engaged in a common task. Liturgy is 'the common prayer of the Church', in which 'the individual drops into place as a member of the worshipping body'. See A. G. Hebert, *Liturgy and Society*, London: Faber and Faber, 1935, p. 64.

2 See Christopher J. Ellis, *Gathering: A Theology and Spirituality of Worship in Free Church Tradition*, London: SCM Press, 2005.

3 Some 72 per cent of Methodist Churches have communion 'less than once a month'. See the Methodist Conference Report, *His Presence Makes the Feast: Holy Communion in the Methodist Church*, Peterborough: Methodist Publishing House, 2003, p. 17. The Report also remarks that 'in the first century of Methodism, 1740–1840, it was not the custom to celebrate communion every week in most parish churches' (p. 6).

4 This growth is evident in, for example, *Seeds in Holy Ground* by the Affairs Committee of the General Synod, London: Archbishops' Council, 2005, pp. 19–23.

5 A similar phenomenon occurred in the nineteenth century, when the male and ordained domination of the main-line churches opened up to the non-ordained and often female members other highly significant pieces of Christian 'work'. A large number of religious women, excluded from ordained sacramental ministry, became novelists, social pioneers and, of course, writers of some of our best-loved hymns.

6 See the many volumes by David Hilton published by Christian Education Publications, most recently *Called to Praise* (Birmingham, 2005). See also Hannah Ward and Jennifer Wild (eds), *Human Rites: Worship Resources for an Age of Change*, London: Mowbray, 1995.

7 See Arthur Cochrane, *Eating and Drinking with Jesus*, Philadelphia, PA: Westminster Press, 1974. The custom of celebrating Eucharist with a real meal has been pursued within the Ashram Community. See the 'Meal Time Eucharist', in John Vincent (ed.), *Community Worship 2000*, Sheffield: Ashram Press (178 Abbeyfield Road, Sheffield S4 7AY), 1999, pp. 16–18.

8 On the earliest 'Coming Together' in New Testament times, see Wayne Meeks, *The First Urban Christians*, New Haven, CT: Yale University Press, 1983, pp. 142–50; Martin D. Stringer, *A Sociological History of Christian Worship*, Cambridge: Cambridge University Press, 2005, pp. 30–6.

9 See Methodist Conference Report, *His Presence Makes the Feast*, pp. 44–7.

10 On 'local liturgy', see the comments on popular religion by Robert J. Schreiter, *Constructing Local Theologies*, Maryknoll, NY: Orbis Books, 1985, pp. 141–3.

11 See Peter Brierley, 'Survey of British Churches' (2004). Philip Richter et al., *Mission-shaped Church*, London: Church House Publishing, 2004, p. 37.

12 On SICEM, see John Vincent, *Hope from the City*, Peterborough: Epworth Press, 2000, pp. 26–35.

13 The description in the next five paragraphs is by Grace Vincent, and slightly updates that in 'Worship in Grimesthorpe', in Chris Rowland and John Vincent (eds), *Liberation Spirituality*, Sheffield: Urban Theology Unit (210 Abbeyfield Road, Sheffield S4 7AZ), 1999, pp. 68–73, especially p. 69.

14 Grace Vincent, 'Worship in Grimesthorpe', p. 73.

15 *Community Worship 2000* (see note 7 above).

16 John Vincent, *Journey: Explorations into Discipleship* (course material in four books), Sheffield: Ashram Press, 2002–2004.

17 On the Ashram Community, see further Eurig Scandrett, Helen Tomlinson and John Vincent, *Journeying with Ashram*, Sheffield: Ashram Press, 2005.

18 See *Community Worship 2000*.

19 See the discussion of 'Conventional Traditions' and 'Radical Traditions', in John Vincent, *Radical Christianity: A Manifesto and Guidebook*, Sheffield: Ashram Press, 2005, pp. 10–13.

20 The present 'Local Ecumenical Partnerships' and 'Shared Churches Agreements' are steps in the right direction, but too often end up with small experimental groups from different denominations who are trying to work together being burdened with wholly unnecessary extra layers of bureaucratic outside control, monitoring or restriction – and being vulnerable to the withdrawal of one or other of their sponsoring denominations.

21 *The Cities: A Methodist Report*, London: NCH, 1997, p. 225.

22 Interestingly, the otherwise highly organized and impeccably liturgically correct (but little used) nine Orders for Holy Communion in *The Methodist Worship Book* (Peterborough: Methodist Publishing House, 1999, pp. 114–220) are followed by a 'structure' for an extempore Eucharist, 'Guidance for Ordering a Service of Holy Communion' (pp. 221–2).

Part 2

WINDOWS INTO FAITH

4

Seeing with God's eyes

MARTIN WALLACE

Context is everything

As I thundered south on the M1 to stay with relatives, my mind was full of all the things I was experiencing back at home, an industrial redevelopment area of Sheffield (now totally disappeared under Meadowhall Retail Park and the Don Valley Sports Arena). Uppermost in my thoughts were the gunshot holes in my windows, my hedge set ablaze, children urinating through the letterbox and adolescents doing the same on my settee. There were the broken car springs caused by youths who jumped on to the boot as I turned a corner, and the bricks coming over our yard wall, missing my baby's pram by inches. My asthma, a direct result of industrial pollution, was playing up and I was exhausted because in the previous five days I had conducted 21 funerals (the average mortality age was 54, the common cause being bronchial disease).

In that context, the heroic church congregation wanted to meet with a God who was not just an escape to some fantasy peace to help them forget their hours in the steel mills. There the huge furnaces and glowing molten metal with hundreds of scampering workers resembled Bosch's pictures of hell, but nor did they want God reduced to nothing more than an industrial social worker. They wanted realistic engagement but with a vision for this life based on our vision of heaven.

Arriving in rural Devon, I found my relatives totally unable to comprehend my concerns, but obsessed with the fact that their ditch was overflowing with slurry from the chicken farm next door, and by the new barn erected by another farmer which was obliterating their view of the green countryside which rolled towards the sparkling blue sea. On Sunday in church, the retired vicar spoke in lilting tones about the love of God, quoting erudite passages from literary authors.

We were like two trains passing each other on adjacent tracks, going in different directions. Neither could understand or identify with the other. Each of us was honestly engaging with the issues of our contexts and in our two churches the worship, message, and congregational life honestly reflected local life, but ultimately of course offered totally different understandings of God's character and mission.

Subsequent ministries in wealthy Surrey with exhausted city financiers, in east London with parents struggling with failing schools and racial tension, and in remote villages with people who had constantly moved 'further out' but discovered in the end you can escape everything and everyone except yourself, have all convinced me that our context governs us more than we ever admit. This, in turn, has helped me to understand the Bible.

Take the Old Testament. The fiery and noisy God who gave ten strict commandments to Moses was naturally found on the harsh and dramatic volcanic Mount Sinai (Exodus 20.1–21). David's Psalm with its experience of God as the personal carer flows easily from the experience of a reflective shepherd boy (Psalm 23). Elijah's 'take-it or leave-it' expression of faith culminating in the contest on Mount Carmel with the Baal prophets is natural from someone whose second home was the rocky desert (1 Kings 18.16–46). Isaiah's experience of a holy God surrounded by cherubim and seraphim feels quite expected from someone who frequented the Temple in Jerusalem (Isaiah 6.1–13). Hosea's message of the God who comes after us even when we publicly humiliate him is especially clear when it comes from the mouth of a betrayed husband buying back his adulterous wife (Hosea 1—3). And so we could go on.

In the gospels, Jesus' words change tone according to where he is. When in the softer, greener hills of Galilee, his message is more inviting and intriguing with his stories about sowers (Luke 8.1–15), lamp stands (Luke 11.33–36), mustard seeds (Luke 13.18–21), wise builders (Matthew 7.24–29), lost sheep (Luke 15.1–7), and coins and children (Luke 15.8–32). But once in the rockier south, in and around Jerusalem, the talk similarly becomes harder and stonier. 'Woe to you', he says seven times (Matthew 23 and 24). The talk is of judgement, the end of the age, the separation of sheep and goats, lazy servants being excluded from the feast. Context has moulded people differently. The issues and the approach needed are different.

Similarly, the epistles demonstrate the same fact. The same Paul writes the epistles, but the different contexts demand different emphases, which if taken separately can appear at odds with each other. The letter to the Colossians would suggest that Christ is Lord not just of the Church but of creation (Colossians 1.15–17: 'by him all things were created: things in heaven and on earth, visible and invisible, whether thrones or powers or rulers or authorities . . . in him all things hold together'). This Jesus is magnificent, distant, and on the throne of heaven. Jesus is a kind of cosmic glue that holds the entire universe together with a priority of our social organization. In contrast, the letter to the Philippians encourages a more intimate and personal spirituality (Philippians 1.6: 'he who began a good work in you will carry it on to completion'). This message is about a Jesus who deliberately left the glory of heaven to become our servant! Taken separately, they seem at odds with each other, but taken together, of course, they present two complementary ministries of Christ. Colossae and Philippi were two different contexts that demanded different theologies of Jesus Christ. Simply to transfer one theology, one understanding, from one context to another and impose it, will inevitably risk imposing an alien theology and thereby an inappropriate spirituality.

We could suggest exactly the same point about the mistakes made by more recent European missionaries to Africa or India who in taking the gospel abroad confused faith and culture. They took their Bibles, but also Western dress, middle-class morality, a theology of the Enlightenment, British hymn books and prayer books – the list is endless.

The fact is that our spirituality is always a constantly reshaping river flowing between the banks of, on one side, our current experience of where we are, and on the other side, our understanding of our scriptural roots, from which we humbly try to learn from others who have gone before us.

Seen like this, our worship, prayers, songs, drama, and liturgy, can never remain fixed for very long, since every year we change according to where we are. Our eyes feed our souls and our souls affect the way our eyes see. Our liturgy cannot be anything other than an expression of how *in this place* we see God, and how *in this place* we think God might see us.

Praying with the Old Testament

Let us take the Psalms as an example. In churches where cathedral-like liturgy is used, the Psalms are often chanted, not infrequently by cherubic choirs with scrubbed faces, dressed in starched white surplices. The tunes follow a style that can easily be followed, but only once you have been admitted to the elite who understand pointing, breathing and rhythm. In this rarefied environment the awful fact is that the words can be sung in such a way as to render them, at best, unusual, and, at worst, unintelligible: 'Lord, grant us thy salvaysion!' I am being harsh, but to caricature this method of using the Psalms is a good example. The fact is that in many Anglican churches, Psalms will be used, either chanted, sung or said, but with little understanding of their origins or application to today's real context.

Similarly, in most Anglican churches, intercessions will be offered which are either read from a book (a great shame) or carefully composed by a member of the congregation. They will be honed and shaped even in the most charismatic or evangelical church. Politically we will be urged to pray for 'guidance' at a general election, rather than be asked to say 'Amen' to a prayer urging God to ensure that the Liberal Democrats will get in to teach the other two parties a lesson (which is probably what a third of the congregation are secretly praying!).

Such intercessions will follow guidelines: for the Church, the world, the local situation, those who are ill, and the bereaved. The contents will probably simply follow the latest news headlines. Thus, without realizing it, the intercessions are allowing the media to decide what millions each Sunday will pray about – and the media themselves have their own criteria for deciding what to include in each day's news. So we have prayers which are both sanitized and not personally rooted.

However, when we turn to the Psalms, what do we find? Certainly not comforting, non-disturbing, politically correct, careful literature. We find dialogue with doubt ('men say to me all day long, "Where is your God?" ' [Psalm 42]); loneliness and despair ('by the rivers of Babylon we sat and wept' [Psalm 137]); and anger ('if only you would slay the wicked, O God' [Psalm 139]). There is questioning ('what are mere mortals that you are mindful of them' [Psalm 8]); fear ('do not hand me over to the desire of my foes' [Psalm 27]); and rejection ('I cried out to God for help . . . has his unfailing love vanished for ever?' [Psalm 77]). There is comfort too ('I sought the LORD and he answered me' [Psalm 34]); love ('his love endures for ever' [Psalm 107]); and constancy ('The LORD is faithful to all his promises' [Psalm 145]). There are songs of pilgrimage ('My soul yearns for the courts of the LORD' [Psalm 84]); journeying to justice ('pray for the peace of Jerusalem' [Psalm 122]); and pleas for a fresh start ('wash away all my iniquity and cleanse me from my sin' [Psalm 51]).

The point is that the Psalms are real – originally from the hearts of real people in real contexts. Some are from David's time, others, no doubt, from subsequent centuries and places; but they are heart-felt. The depths of emotion are there, as are the real issues of the day and the feelings of the author – captivity, attack, exile, resentment, anger, depression, lethargy, joy, love, friendship, release – the list is endless.

Not only are they full of emotion, as much emotion as is ex-pressed in the kitchen or the pub or the office, but they are full of question marks. They are not neat and tidy – and dare I say it, certainly not designed to be chanted carefully. Many demand to be shouted, and feel like a real conversation, sometimes almost an argument, with God.

So what does this disjunction between the Psalms we say we value, and our current all-too-often style of intercession say about us and how we see each other and how we see God? Could it reveal that we find it pretty impossible to be honest in church since our private prayers probably bear almost no relationship to the careful sentiments expressed in church? Is it that we are afraid of upsetting each other with our direct petitions about who should be our Prime Minister? Is it that we are afraid of exploring our own doubts about God, our own anxieties about what the boss might say tomorrow, and our own sense of loneliness, because we do not really trust each other as God's family? Is it that we are afraid to reveal the sort of God we really believe in, the God we pray to privately in our bedroom, car, toilet or office?

What would next Sunday be like if we prayed, really prayed, in the style of the Psalms? We would begin with our actual context, not that dictated by the media. We would pray from our heart, and not from a book that is inevitably from someone else's heart and context. We would pray with difficult questions and sometimes be prepared to leave it at that rather than wrap it up smoothly:

> Lord, when I walk alone under the railway arches, I am scared
> witless . . .
> I look up my street and think, where on earth can I get any
> help . . .
> If my foot slips on the ladder while I'm carrying a heavy load of
> bricks, I really need to ask you to hold me up, Lord . . .
> Lord, when will they learn? . . .
> No one appreciates the ironing I do. I feel left on the rubbish
> heap . . .
> Praise the Lord all Jubilee Terrace, Railway Cuttings and London
> Road . . .
> To know your peace is like the nice warm bath I had last night . . .
> Lord, what on earth are you doing with the weather? . . .
> Praise God all you birds and fishes, drainpipes and gutters, shops
> and houses . . .
> . . . and bring those murderous killers to justice soon . . . !

Such praying from the heart, and from the context, confronts directly our liturgical practice of reading in services a particular psalm just because that is the one set for the day. It is not that learning the psalm has no value (just the opposite!), but that they exist to be used when we are in a state of heart and a context that makes a particular psalm appropriate.

Praying with the New Testament

Let us take as an example my favourite book. In the last book of the Bible, Revelation, we have the series of visions given to a man called John who, around the end of the first century, was a political prisoner in exile working in the rock quarries on the island of Patmos near Turkey. They are quite remarkable: a series of pictures beginning with Jesus as he is in glory (Chapter 1), moving on to seven messages given to seven typically struggling churches (Chapters 2 and 3), and then to a fantastic picture of the worship enjoyed by those who are in heaven (Chapter 4). We then move on to an unfolding of the layers of what spiritual forces are at work in creation, and it climaxes with a vision of God's dream for all of us – nothing less than heaven itself (Chapter 22.1–5). It is an experience in which everything and everyone is whole and free from any sort of decay. This is God's Kingdom, his rule, which comes upon us in part in this life, and thus gives a clue about the eternal destiny God desires for all of us.

In this picture gallery God sits publicly on his throne, acknowledged and worshipped (Chapter 22.1), whereas in reality I recall the man in church one evening who, every time he mentioned the magistrate in the court he had just left, pointed to the altar, the symbol of an out-of-touch judge; and the man who said he could not come to church because it reminded him of school – 'stand when teacher enters, sit when told, get books out, be told off, then go!' They were not prepared to relive an experience of autocratic authority and failure. Our liturgical framework stopped both of them 'seeing' God at all as someone to be freely and lovingly worshipped on his throne!

Revelation speaks of the clear water of the Spirit flowing freely through the street (Chapter 22.1–2). But I know of roads which constantly subside through crumbling ancient sewers after years of neglect, and from which dirty water flows in and out of sight. Instead of Heaven's tree of life with leaves for the healing of the nations (Chapter 22.2), the trees are few in number, vandalized and surrounded by canine deposits. Different ethnic groups find not healing but distrust, victimization and discrimination in shops, in crowds, at work and at school. Verbal, cultural and physical battle is the order of the day.

In Heaven, nothing is under a curse (Chapter 22.3), but much that is under God's curse is to be found in society: personal selfishness (lying to climb the housing ladder); greed (sale of stolen goods); immorality (child abuse and drug peddling); institutionalized crime (social exclusion by insurance agencies and employers who are guided by postal codes); and social deprivation of all sorts.

In Heaven, free worship comes from easily and publicly identified believers (Chapter 22.4), whereas on earth Christians who wish not to work on Sunday are penalized. In Heaven, there is 'no night' (Chapter 22.5), but on earth a great deal of shadowy activity goes on in the office where business deals are clinched, time-sheets are fiddled, income tax is evaded, and women are abused. Vast numbers work under conditions that cause disease and disability as people find themselves working longer and harder with fewer resources to produce more – and even if a target is reached, the next year that target has 5 per cent added so the pressure never eases. No wonder the greatest cause of death of 16–24-year-old males (the very years they enter employment) is suicide, and we are prescribing more anti-depressants than ever.

Praying with the New Testament, means praying with it open and praying in stereo – trying to make an orchestrated symphony of God's ideal and what we actually have. That means praying in such a way that there is no dichotomy between our verbal prayers and our physical life. So, we cannot pray for those starving in Africa without both financially giving and politically agitating for change. We cannot pray about important environmental or economic or housing decisions unless we are actively involved in bringing about the changes necessary. For some, this will mean joining a political party, or pressure group; for others it will mean campaigning locally; for others it might mean offering support as a carer or befriender; and for others it might involve moving house to a less affluent area to identify with and give hope to people, or changing jobs to where we have a greater social effect in what we are doing.

The point is that it is only when our reflections on the offering of the biblical authors (like John) meet our honest observation of what is going on around us that our prayers can become earthed. And they only become real when we become part of the answer to our own prayers – to God's yearning for creation. Then our liturgy is not just an expression of how we see God, ourselves and society, but our liturgy (our work) becomes the visible action that enables others also to see God, themselves and society as he sees, and moreover, enables us to see what is his dream for us all. In short, it is what fires us to work so that the kingdoms of earth reflect nothing less than the Kingdom of Heaven.

Praying from observation

At the beginning of the Bible we are taken into the Garden of Eden (Genesis 2.1–25). In that Garden, and in intimate imagery, we are presented with a picture of God seeing what happened with Adam and Eve and then walking in the garden in the cool of the evening. He met with the couple and they discussed the situation together. The rest of the Bible is the steady progress from that ideal garden, through centuries of history, to the ideal city of heaven, New Jerusalem (Revelation 22).

This is done through pictorial presentations which seem quite normal in the Bible. Visions and dreams were part of life. Joseph dreamed of seven cows and ears of corn (Genesis 41), Isaiah saw a vision of God while in the temple (Isaiah 6), Joel spoke of young and old seeing dreams and visions (Joel 2), Peter had the vision of a sheet holding food (Acts 10), and Paul saw a visionary man beckoning him to new lands (Acts 16.9–10). Visually enacted prophecy was the life-blood of Hosea whose whole message was bound up with his own disastrous marriage (Hosea 1—3), and Jeremiah smashed pottery to make his point (Jeremiah 19). With each of these, the visions or visual presentations were suggested by what was seen, and then used by God.

The parables of Jesus are similarly drawn from visual observation, and his miracles at the very least are visually dramatic presentations of God's love and power. His temptations in the wilderness sprung from reflections on what he saw – stones, a precipice and a panoramic view (Matthew 4.1–11). At his baptism there was the vision of a dove (Matthew 3.16), at his transfiguration there was the vision of Moses and Elijah (Matthew 17.1–13) and at both the voice of God.

My own personal Christian journey has been punctuated in this way. At the age of 17, my faith became personally real when I had a very powerful vision of Jesus on the cross and realized that the nails in his hand were a sign of his love for me. My call into ordained ministry a year later was the result of a vision of God on heaven's throne calling me by name. The move to my first parish came about because of a scene in a dream that I realized matched exactly what I saw in one of the parishes I explored. So it goes on – my latest move to the Diocese of York was the result of a response to my request for a sign that involved a visit to a church I had no previous knowledge of, only to find it an exact replica of York Minster's Chapter House!

The fact is that God uses our eyes and our imagination. We are not designed to be purely cerebral in our decision-making, pilgrimage through life, choice of priorities, or ways of relating to each other or to him. Moreover, to think in this visual way is not weird or unduly mystical, but very earthy.

The picture may be one which helps us to understand Jesus' sacrifice:

I sit in the traffic queue
Low in my car
Next to the huge wheel of a bus.
Large, round, black, rubber, tyre.
Without that tyre the journey will be impaired.
It is that, and that alone
Which connects the bus to the road.

Connections are your business, Lord.
You sent Jesus
To connect earth to heaven
        humanity to divinity
        creature to creator
        death to life
        everyday life to spiritual truth.

As the journey proceeds
So that tyre is bruised, crushed, worn and punctured,
So was Jesus.
Connections involve such suffering and self-giving.
Mediation they call it.

Thoughts
From a bus tyre.

(Martin Wallace, *City Prayers*)[1]

It may cause us to reflect on our own lives:

I stare across the kitchen table
At the vivid crimson of the ketchup bottle.
It reminds me, Lord, that
My 'Sins are red as scarlet',
According to your servant Isaiah.
Just as red screams 'danger' in the mind,
Or 'stop' at traffic lights,
Or 'help' as I cut my finger,
So my sins scream out to you:
The lies, the cheating, the selfishness,
The resentment and unforgiving thoughts.
My sheer rebellion against your love
Is violent red.

I know too of another red
The red that flowed from his hands and his feet,
From his head and his side,

As Jesus hung on the cross:
That deep red blood that alone gives me life –
Eternal life.
Your son was given that I might live.
His red
Covers
My red.
You have spoken to me Lord
Of the important things of life
From a ketchup bottle.

(Martin Wallace, City Prayers)

It may lead us to pray for those people easily forgotten:

Lord, I'm sure you see dear old Elsie
Sitting all day behind her curtains
Watching the world go by.
She thinks she is hidden
Behind the thick nets,
But all is revealed.

Long ago you tore a curtain from top to bottom
To reveal the Holy of Holies in the Temple
When your Son Jesus died.

Your apostle John on the island of Patmos
Saw you draw the curtain back
On the window of Heaven,
And witnessed what was indeed a Revelation.

Lord you are in the business
Of drawing back the curtains.
Please help Elsie to draw back the curtains
So she may be seen to be seen
And so be free to wave and smile –
To reveal and to be revealed.
For in that meeting
In that revelation
There may be
Holiness.

(Martin Wallace, City Prayers)

It may help us value those we take for granted:

You have accompanied me to the hairdresser, Lord,
And we watch the locks fall to the floor.

53

Years ago in Corinth
Paul told the women in the church
To keep their hair covered.
Some say because hair displayed loose
Symbolised a loose woman.
Others say because in a newly mixed congregation
The men couldn't concentrate.
Either way, Lord, hair affected communion
Between you and between people.
Centuries earlier Samson had discovered
Exactly the same lesson.

In a strange way here too, Lord,
The hairdresser is a focus of communion.
Not necessarily with you
But certainly with the soul.
For souls are bared,
Opinions, experiences and feelings are shared.
The hairdresser is the acknowledged, untrained,
Social counsellor.
And in a mysterious way
Unknown to himself
He and his trade
Are doing something
Quite holy.

(Martin Wallace, *City Prayers*)

Or it may lead to a hard challenge:

These Christians tell me, Lord,
They will send their child
To a school out of this area
Because education there is 'better'
In a more affluent community.

They do not care that they are robbing their neighbour
And their school
Of their child
Who is a witness to the world,
That you care for this place.
For they are only concerned
About the progress of the members
Of their own isolated family.

Lord, you so loved the world
That you gave your only child.

The sending of one's child
To the local school
For the sake of this place
Is living the Gospel.
Actions speak so much louder
Than words, Lord.
Thank you for giving us your Son.

(Martin Wallace, *City Prayers*)

To see those around through the eyes of faith, and to see Scripture with the sights of those around, changes dramatically how we see God, and just may reflect how we think he sees us.

Praying with a glint in the eye

The Iona Community produce wonderfully startling prayers. Some years ago in the daily prayers came a superb example which ran along the lines of:

Lord, I am fed up with sour, dour, Christians.
Please give us joy and happiness and laughter.
But not the sort of hysterical laughter you gave to Sarai,
Abraham's wife,
When you made her pregnant at the age of ninety!

In church, it is lovely to see a prayer that is clearly designed to bring a smile to the face, and to break the stiffness of a corporate act of worship. In the same way, outside the church it is fun to see the humour of bygone ages on headstones in churchyards:

Here lie the bones of Elizabeth Charlotte,
Born a virgin, died a harlot.

Such examples remind us that we have a sense of humour, and if we are made in the image of God then, presumably, he has a sense of humour too. Humour cannot be kept to ourselves, it is for sharing. God is community – Father, Son and Holy Spirit – and if we are built in his image, then we too must be designed for community and for sharing. The conclusion must be that while private prayer is perfectly good, corporate worship – and worship with a smile – are also perfectly good.

When God created the heavens and the earth from the waters of the deep (Genesis 1.1–2) and did it by speaking (Genesis 1.3, 6, 9, 11, 14, 20, 24, 26), maybe his word was spoken as a joyful act of laughter. Did God smile as he spoke, and did the raucous breath (Spirit) of his creativity disturb the waters and so bring things into being with joy and with the intention that we should enjoy life and enjoy him? I like to think so.

Scholars with humourless minds agonize about precisely what Jesus meant by phrases such as: 'It is easier for a camel to pass through the eye of a needle than for a rich man to enter the kingdom of heaven' (Mark 10.25). They ask, 'Did the eye of a needle refer to a side gate in the wall of Jerusalem?' No – it was just plain funny! Or what about Jesus' question: 'Why do you look at the speck of sawdust in your brother's eye and pay no attention to the plank in your own?' (Matthew 7.3)? At the time, the crowds would have fallen about with this example of overstated 'alternative' comedy. It is only our churchy repetition that has dulled the impact for us – and our tendency to approach Scripture with an unduly humourless mind.

Jesus suggested often that the Kingdom of God is a party: 'How is it your disciples do not fast?' (Matthew 9.14); 'there were twelve basketfuls of bread' *left over* from the feeding of the five thousand (Matthew 14.20); 'the Kingdom of Heaven is like a king who prepared a wedding banquet' (Matthew 22.2); 'I will not drink of this fruit of the vine from now until the day when I drink it again with you in my Father's Kingdom' (Matthew 26.29) – and so on.

There is a lovely prayer from a tenth-century Celtic monk:

> I would like to have the people of heaven
> In my own house:
> With vats of good cheer
> Laid out for them.
>
> I would like to have all the saints,
> Their fame is so great.
> I would like people
> From every corner of heaven.
>
> I would like them to be cheerful
> In their drinking.
> I would like to have Jesus too
> Here amongst them.

I would like a great lake of beer
For the King of Kings,
I would like to be watching heaven's family
Drinking it through all eternity.
    (Martin Wallace, *Pocket Celtic Prayer*)[2]

Urban people understand all this instinctively. The anthem of West Ham Football Club is 'I'm forever blowing bubbles'. It is a way of saying, 'whatever hardships are thrown at us, we are quite capable of blowing a raspberry at it and carrying on regardless'. That is why the television serial *EastEnders* misses the mark so widely. It is so appallingly depressing and badly unrealistic since nowhere in the cast is there the joker every crowd has. No pub survives without laughter, jokes and leg-pulling – the Queen Vic is simply unreal!

While I was a vicar in one parish, there were times when we organized 'Cabaret Services'. These were an attempt to forget the inherited tradition of church services and return to the atmosphere of the feeding of the five thousand (Mark 6.30–44). There Jesus did not tell people to sit in rows, get hymn books out, turn to page 43 of the service book, and look glum. Rather, the people sat in groups informally, ate and drank, met with Jesus, were taught by him, and returned home refreshed. This seemed very similar to the approach of a cabaret club evening out: people sit around tables with food and drink, the entertainment is interactive (and it has to be good to retain the attention over the noise!), and people go home different and happy.

These Cabaret Services were held in dim lighting, with people sitting around low tables. Food and drink were served throughout. The lesson would be a large-screen video clip from, say, *Jesus of Nazareth*, and the sermon would be in the style of a roving comedian interacting with any number of individuals in the congregation. Prayers would be encouraged in small groups around the tables. Drama would be integral, and the songs would be sung karaoke-style from a large screen with words composed to tunes we knew well from the television, pop or 'easy listening' charts, or folk tunes. The proof of the pudding lay in the result that many came to these services who did not regularly come to church, simply because we had taken the normal elements of our liturgy but adapted their presentation to the local culture and not been too straight-faced about it.

Then there were our Celebration Weekends set in an area where literacy was not uniformly high. They were wonderful times of fun, laughter and creativity. There were hymns composed to currently popular tunes, modern prayers of anguish or questioning using local imagery written in the style of the ancient Psalms, and t-shirt printing was offered with home-grown designs of a Christian flavour. Broken coloured glass was used to create stained-glass windows, comedy workshops were led by a professional comic, advertisement posters would be drawn, calligraphy of texts would be offered, flower arranging was assumed, a huge 10-ft by 6-ft mural would be painted corporately, and there would be dance, drama, origami, video-making, banners, cake decorating, an orchestra, badge-making and so on. And all actively completed during a wonderful climactic service of celebration uniting around themes such as new birth, the Holy Spirit, or the City of God.

None of this is a denial of the harshness and struggle of much urban life. It is rather a corrective to the often too-furrowed brows of the middle-class do-gooders who come in as social workers, teachers or clergy, and then live off telling everyone how awful life is in deprived areas, but fail to bring alive the innate inner resources God gives everyone. Such people are little more than 'urban pimps', living off the misery of others (perhaps even writing their books about it!), and missing the point of how God sees us and wants us to see both ourselves and him.

Conclusion

Worship as the 'window of the urban church' (or any other church, come to that) is thus about:

- recognizing and affirming that God works through and in the place where we are;
- praying in a way which is as honest as the Bible itself;
- allowing the biblical vision to break through our prayers into action;
- offering our imagination to God so that mere words do not restrict his dealings with us;
- enjoying God's company as he seeks to transform society.

Perhaps these two images help:

- It is not about trying to push God's finger to point where we think it should. Rather it is about sitting on God's finger to see where he is pointing. But more than that –

- It is about seeing the people and places to which he is pointing and recognizing that he wants to bring laughter and joy where it is in short supply. He wants to 'wipe every tear from their eyes . . . and abolish death, mourning, crying and pain, for the old order has passed away' (Revelation 21.4).

The blessing of Aaron (Numbers 6.25) could then be paraphrased:

> The Lord bless you and keep you;
> the Lord make his face to smile and beam on you;
> the Lord look kindly on you
> and give you his peace.

Notes

1 Martin Wallace, *City Prayers*, Norwich: Canterbury Press, 1995.
2 Martin Wallace, *Pocket Celtic Prayer*, London: Church House Publishing, 1996.

5

Apt liturgy: to lift eyes above the horizon

ANN MORISY AND ANN JEFFRIES

For those who remember chortling at the *Morecambe and Wise Christmas Special*, the antics of Matt Lucas and David Walliams in *Little Britain* can come as a shock. *Little Britain* offers a merciless parody of the eccentricities and hypocrisies of postmodern Britain. However, it does this by purveying breath-taking crudity. What makes us laugh has clearly changed over the past 30 years. The preoccupation with earthy and biological processes is now a characteristic of mass culture. We are engrossed by our creatureliness and only rarely set our sights above the mundane. Thoughts of ultimacy, perceptions of holiness and visions of human flourishing have become a foreign land for so many of us. In such a context, apt liturgy[1] is a subversive process.

Apt liturgy invites people to lift their eyes above the horizon and respond to that aspect of our humanity which is beyond our creatureliness. However, to be effective, such an invitation has to take account of how we have not just lost our awareness of the realms of ultimacy and the holy, we have also forgotten how to get there. It is rather to the point therefore that a recent study in Plymouth revealed that residents in a neighbourhood of serious multiple deprivation expressed anger that they did not have the words to even talk about this other dimension that they sensed was missing in their lives.[2]

Recognizing that churches can be daunting places for the uninitiated to enter, another feature of apt liturgy is that often it does not require people to cross the threshold of a church. It may take place on a street corner where there has been a road death, or in the park where there has been a stabbing. It has occurred in a mini-bus taking an old people's club to visit places to which they had been

60

evacuated during the war and, in a more upbeat mode, in a coach taking the local marching band to the regional championships. However, apt liturgies generally tend to be short and simple. The liturgy in the mini-bus mentioned above took eight minutes yet was grounded in the complex emotions arising from the participants' memories. The minister then made links between the war that had engulfed London 50 years ago and the experience of war facing people in other countries today and concluded her prayers by thanking God for his son Jesus who also died for the sake of others. Another minister who created an apt liturgy for a debt advice project concluded this liturgy by thanking God who through his son waived everyone's debts.

In Plymouth, the Halcyon Neighbourhood Centre based in the hall at Halcyon Methodist Church and run by the Action Group for Halcyon, which includes community and church members, had a week-long celebration of talents focusing on the contributions that local people made to the work of the Centre. At the end of the week everyone was invited to join in a simple celebration of talents in the Church. During the celebration, participants' experiences were acknowledged; their struggles and their contributions were recognized; links were made between their experience and that of others and a deeper sense of solidarity created. Finally, the relevance of Scripture and the alongsideness of God were suggested.[3] The positive responses from people who never usually came to church were significant, perhaps because what was kindled through the celebration countered preoccupation with the mundane individualism that hardens the habits of the heart.

Apt more than contextual

Apt liturgies arise out of the events that occur in people's daily lives. The events which are the focus for apt liturgy are akin to the idea of pericopes (self-contained unit of biblical text).[4] Just as biblical scholars often focus on pericopes as self-contained units of text, so too the creation of apt liturgy requires the identification of a similar 'self-contained' and shared event. The term 'apt' liturgy is therefore preferred to that of 'contextual' liturgy because it emphasizes the idea that the liturgy is associated with an event, whereas 'contextual' carries wider connotations of location or sub-culture or fashion. The event on which apt liturgy focuses is one which concerns a community, a city or even a nation. In this way, it is distinguished from the 'occasional offices' such as baptism, marriage or a funeral, which are clearly events, but most often they are events which preoccupy family and friends rather than a wider network.

Very often, apt liturgy is triggered by the shocking deaths, death which moves beyond the personal into the public domain. The village of Soham – and people wider afield – were shocked at the murder of two teenage schoolgirls, Jessica Chapman and Holly Wells. The people of Huyton in Merseyside were shocked by the racist murder of Anthony Walker. Even in a world where thoughts of ultimacy rarely penetrate, most of us remain inclined towards friendship with God when forced to live our daily lives 'with death in our eye'.[5] Unsurprisingly therefore, one of the early manifestations of apt liturgy was prompted by the slaughter of millions in war.

The Unknown Warrior

World War I left between 9 and 13 million combatants dead, perhaps as many as one-third of them with no known grave. The Reverend David Railton MC, who had served as a padre in France in 1916, had the idea that the body of an unknown soldier, sailor or airman, be returned to England for burial in Westminster Abbey, to symbolise all those who had died for their country but whose place of death was not known.

On the morning of 11 November 1920 the coffin with the Unknown Warrior was drawn in a procession on a gun carriage pulled by six black horses, first to the Cenotaph in London and then on to Westminster Abbey. Many of the people who lined the streets to watch the cortège pass had been waiting all night. The body of the Unknown Warrior, followed by the King and ministers of state, was borne to the west end of the nave through a guard of honour of 100 holders of the Victoria Cross, and here the burial service was held.

The organisers were taken completely by surprise by the response of the people to the ceremony. At least 40,000 people passed through the Abbey before the doors were closed that night. The pilgrimage went on throughout the weekend, with Saturday bringing large numbers of pilgrims from outside London. Up to the time the tomb was closed a week later, an estimated 1,250,000 people visited the Abbey.[6]

Apt liturgy is often devised or prompted by death or extreme destructiveness[7] because it is the challenge of making sense of death – or of making sense of human wickedness – or frailness that focuses the thoughts on the possibility of eternity. And in pondering on the possibility of eternity a host of other metaphysical issues follow in its wake. Yet apt liturgy does not have as its aim the promotion of a systematic Christian teaching: rather, the aim is to engage with the rough, unresolved and often disconcerting emotions that are aroused by the unfairness and poignancy that are so often provoked by untimely or extensive loss of life. Apt liturgy therefore is a distinctive and timely offering in response to the loneliness and distress of the ordinarily earth-bound human selves, in our corporate hour of need.

Pastoral and missional

When apt liturgy is created around the distress associated with grievous death, it is first and foremost a pastoral response. It aims to help people to better face the world with an enhanced sense of solidarity and hope, shifting unbearable pain from one back to the backs of many. Yet apt liturgy also serves to create a foundation for faith, for it will inevitably endeavour to give confidence in the possibility of 'God with us', i.e. the profound reality of the incarnation of God.

The challenge of apt liturgy is to help people to see beyond the routine, mundane consciousness of everyday life and discover that within our ordinary experiences there are rumours of angels and traces of ultimacy. John O'Donohue describes this as 'a ministry of awakening, helping people to see beyond the daily round of worldly commitment, to awaken in them a sense of their eternal origin and destiny'.[8] Without this awakening, it is difficult to see how a foundation for the nurturing of faith can be achieved. Apt liturgy can also create a 'memory of the heart', i.e. ideas and images that can be pondered and drawn on over time as well as provide symbols and stories that 'waft us heavenward'. However, pastoral and missional concerns combine powerfully in relation to apt liturgy because, at its heart, apt liturgy desires to give people the courage to open conversation with God and to recommit themselves to a hopeful perspective.

The effectiveness of the pastoral and missional aspect of apt liturgy are consistent with Grace Davie's extensive research[9] into the way contemporary society has developed a 'vicarious' approach to religion whereby the many, who rarely or never attend a church service, nevertheless value the fact that the few, i.e. those who are active churchgoers, maintain religious practice and culture so that they can be a part of it at times of great trauma or significance. A pertinent example was the response in a rural parish in Devon to the outpouring of concern over the tsunami disaster on Boxing Day 2004.

> A vigil was held in the ancient parish church from 6 p.m. to midnight one Saturday in early January 2005 to reflect on, share information about and pray for the victims of manmade and natural disasters in the previous year. Different community members volunteered to come and share their particular knowledge and reflections or their musical and artistic talents – it was truly an offering by and of the people of the parish, most of whom rarely attended regular services.

Apt liturgy is essentially a public event. Indeed, it could be suggested that apt liturgy is the closest the Church comes to the original meaning of the Greek word from which the word 'liturgy' is derived, namely: 'the work of the people'. Yet because it is a public occasion, apt liturgy has to be respectful of people's unbelief and inchoate belief. It offers a space which allows participants[10] autonomy to reflect on events in their own way and is respectful of unbelief – as well as people's capacity for truth seeking. In order to do its work – that of enabling people to face the world better because of a greater sense of solidarity and hope – apt liturgy must also aim to foster within each person an openness to the possibility of God and a renewal of hopefulness.

To summarize, the *distinguishing features* of apt liturgy are:

- It is grounded in people's experience, concerns or dilemmas.
- It acknowledges, articulates and respects strong feelings.
- It promotes a sense of solidarity with and empathy for others.
- It suggests new perspectives, enabling understanding and awareness.
- It provides opportunities for reflection in light of Scripture.
- It develops a sense of the alongsideness of God.
- It introduces basic religious symbols and concepts that can be pondered over time and drawn on.
- It stimulates hope, confidence and the will for renewal and/or action.

Apt liturgy and transformation

Tim Stratford draws on the insights of an Action and Reflection Cycle inspired by Paulo Freire in relation to the weekly discipline of worship. In the context of apt liturgy, Freire's notion of conscientization is also relevant. Conscientization is a term used by Freire[11] to describe the process at the heart of education for liberation or what is sometimes referred to as radical education. For Freire, the process of conscientization involves the 'learner' becoming critically engaged in reviewing his or her world and experiences, challenging taken-for-granted ways of seeing and understanding, resulting in an increased ability to transform reality. The process of conscientization can also bring a sense of solidarity with others and a commitment to action or 'struggle' together in a common cause. The new perspectives and new ways of seeing that emerge in the process of conscientization are similar to the processes that can be set in train through apt liturgy. Indeed, Freire's insights are very much reflected in each of the examples above. The starting point in each example was the lived experience of people in their everyday life. Their experiences and feelings were acknowledged and respected and they were encouraged to reflect for themselves on the connection to the experience of others. Stories from Scripture are offered that connect to the situation and yet also offer solidarity across time and culture – which both reassures and renews, and gives scope for critical awareness to develop.

Apt liturgy has the capacity to renew energy and enable re-commitment to the 'struggle'. For example, Ann Morisy illustrates how apt liturgy could have a special role in relation to hard-pressed communities that face the arduous processes associated with urban regeneration and neighbourhood renewal.[12] Drawing on the insights of Russ Parker[13] and his work on healing wounded history, Morisy suggests that the five stages that Parker identifies as critical to the healing of past hurts experienced by communities can also provide a structure around which apt liturgy can be devised. The five stages that Parker identifies in relation to healing wounded history are:

1 *remembering* in relation to Scripture;
2 *hearing/lamenting* the experiences of those involved;
3 *owning/confessing* our shortcomings in relation to these stories;
4 *repentance/commitment* to a new way;

5 readiness to accept *forgiveness* and *to turn around*, in the sense that future behaviour aims at being different from previous behaviour or action.

By using this five-stage structure, it is possible to 'hold up' community griefs, anger and dismay; strong and troubling emotions can be named and people are enabled to reflect on the event. Apt liturgy can deftly acknowledge past hurts without drifting into blaming or reopening past wounds. In particular, apt liturgy gives public recognition to the fact that everyone is both prone to get things wrong and to do wrong, and that, deep down, everyone knows the reality of both our complicity and vulnerability. This is part of the distinctive 'offering' that is possible because of the Christian assumption that 'all have fallen short'. This is 'normalizing' or acceptance of human failure and fragility, in contrast to the inclination to scapegoat and find fault. This is part of the health-giving nature of apt liturgy. However, apt liturgy also has to kindle hope and commitment to a better future. The twin dynamics of humility and the renewal of hope are essential to the change-orientated action that Freire considers to be the essential culmination of conscientization.

Apt liturgy, in order to carry a sense of hope and the possibility of a fresh start, has to encourage people to 'lift their eyes above the mundane'. Apt liturgy cannot but invite people to ponder the possibility that God is also involved in their struggle for renewal and re-commitment. In this way the apt liturgy also has a role in relation to mission, in that it can provide a foundation for further and more subtle understanding about what is at the heart of the Christian faith. In addition to bringing an implicit acknowledgement that part of being human is to 'mess up' and therefore to need forgiveness and renewal, apt liturgy can help foster a sense of solidarity with others – and invite people to ponder the possibility that God is also in solidarity with this struggle and commitment to make the future better than the past.

Apt liturgy in a multifaith context: an example from Plymouth

Apt liturgy, by definition, is public liturgy. However, within the public domain, people do not just have inchoate or half-formed faith, it is also the locale of people with faiths other that Christianity. As the impact of globalization on cities and towns extends, the public domain becomes more and more 'multifaith'. The challenge therefore is for apt liturgy to be able to deliver its aims in a way which can incorporate the reality of people of other faiths. In trying to accommodate people of other faiths, does the pastoral and missional potential of apt liturgy dissipate? Does apt liturgy to be effective therefore have to be restricted to expression within a single faith? The experience of apt liturgy in Plymouth suggests not.

In Plymouth, a multifaith apt liturgy was devised as part of a process to galvanize support for asylum seekers in the city. The event took place as the culmination of the work undertaken in Plymouth in connection with the national Commission on Urban Life and Faith. A group drawn from across faiths and denominations had been formed to mirror the work of the Commission on Urban Life and Faith in reflecting on 'What makes a good city?' The group was keen to ensure that it did more than generate paper and talk, not least because the priority was to enable 'the voices of the most marginalised to be heard'.[14]

In Plymouth, with these things in mind, the destitution crisis among asylum seekers stood out, and having consulted with those already engaged in supporting asylum seekers in the city, this became the priority for the group. It became clear that few church people knew the nature and extent of the destitution experienced by asylum seekers in the city. The first challenge therefore was to give a platform from which these heart-rending stories could be heard. The group overseeing the process sought the support of the different faith group leaders in Plymouth in order to prepare for a large, multifaith event around this issue. Not only was the aim to galvanize more support and develop greater interfaith understanding, it was also hoped that by doing this, pressure could be brought to bear on decision-makers for more humanitarian policies and procedures.

Remarkably, the event was able to carry out a number of aims:

1 to listen and respond to the voices of these marginalized people;
2 to galvanize greater, more consistent and better co-ordinated support for asylum seekers from members of faith groups;
3 to develop awareness of the way asylum seekers and refugees contribute to the life of the City of Plymouth;

4 to model a way of working that will improve partnership working *between* faith communities and *with* other organizations;

5 to engender participation by members of faith communities in the event;

6 to demonstrate the potential of 'apt liturgy' from a multifaith perspective;

7 to set up a process that will maximize the likelihood of follow-up action;

8 to develop awareness of the resources and unique dimension that faith communities can contribute to the well-being of society.

The event took place at the end of a national election. The campaign leading up to the election had been peppered with muddled, misleading and sometimes racist statements about asylum seekers. This had generated a lot of emotion and heightened the significance of the issue. The challenge therefore was whether people would be sufficiently motivated to come to an event which would clearly aim to present a different perspective to the dominant assumptions. It was deemed crucial to emphasize the significance being given to the event by key people in the city. Therefore, all invitations were sent to named individuals in the name of the Lord Mayor who, as a person of colour himself, had agreed to open the evening.

The components of the evening event proved remarkably consistent with the five stages that Parker suggests are essential to the process of healing wounded history.[15] For example, in opening the evening, the Lord Mayor began by *remembering* Plymouth's long history of both welcoming traders and immigrants from abroad and its confidence in reaching out to far-flung corners of the world, as the final port of embarkation for emigrants. This was followed by a presentation which contrasted negative headlines about asylum seekers and refugees with the reality of the situation. The link with Holy Scripture in this multifaith context involved nine representatives from different faith perspectives simply reciting a verse from their religious text, often initially in its original language. Without exception, all the contributions from the different scriptures called upon their members to welcome the stranger and the presenters reinforced how this was an essential expression of each faith. This first stage ended with a pause for quiet reflection.

The second element of the event, *hearing and lamenting*, took the form of stories detailing experiences of asylum seekers interspersed with more facts aimed at 'myth-busting' to counter the vitriol and misleading information that was so much part of the recent election. To enable participants to be more actively involved in this process, (*owning/confessing*), they were encouraged during the break to read the information in their conference packs, to take part in a quiz (designed to reinforce the information contained in the presentations) and to visit the agency displays. These included the contents of a rough sleeper's pack and a video with more personal stories and portrayal of an eviction of a failed asylum seeker.

Following the break, people had a chance to comment and ask questions of a panel that included members of the asylum seeker and refugee community. Given the bad press during the election, all questions and comments were surprisingly positive. Clearly many were quite shocked at what they had heard and, as had been suspected, quite unaware that such traumatic events were happening in Plymouth. The stress on personal stories throughout the evening proved to be powerful, in the way that Leonie Sandercock suggests is important as cities become more multi-ethnic and multicultural. She suggests that in such contexts, storytelling has to become an urban art, because recounting and hearing different stories from different tellers help people to move out of entrenched positions into more receptive and open frames of mind.[16] In particular, the contrast between the stories shared by asylum seekers of their experiences contrasted dramatically with the behaviour urged by all the major religions as being the measure of faithful behaviour.

In relation to Parker's fourth component, *repentance/commitment*, the event moved on to short presentations as to the specifics of what was needed by local agencies working with asylum seekers and refugees. This provided opportunities to respond as individuals and/or to join working parties to work collaboratively on longer-term solutions to pressing needs such as emergency accommodation. Some asylum seekers who were volunteering with particular agencies were part of these presentations. Here was an opportunity to express solidarity across cultures – the universalizing process which speaks of a willingness to let go of individualism.

The final component of the event involved *forgiveness/action*. Those who came to the event were encouraged to complete commitment slips (some 40 were handed in) and urged to attend a follow-up meeting three weeks later to progress the work. The evening ended with a few moments of reflection and closing words and then a refugee got up and danced, his music saluting the departing participants.

This was a truly moving evening and a huge success. Some 150 people registered but we estimated there were closer to 200 in the hall. As one refugee said 'I have never felt so supported and honoured in Plymouth. Thank you.' The evaluation of the event noted:

> Generally felt to have been very successful both in ambience and content . . . well over 150 people attended from a broad range of faith groups and other agencies . . . The presentations of faith texts from the nine different faith group representatives was agreed to have provided a moving start to the event. Many had commented that they had never been present at anything like that in Plymouth before and were also impressed that they kept to the allotted time! . . . The Guildhall was felt to have been just the right venue and the Mayor's involvement was appreciated. Displays from the 10 different agencies present had been helpful as were the presentations about the destitution crisis . . . The Police Diversity Officer was present as were many from other organisations working with Refugees and Asylum Seekers.

However, those who organized the event knew that the real test would be how many people turned up to the follow-up event which clearly entailed a commitment to get involved. About 70 people attended. While the bulk of the evening was spent working in small groups, the evening was brought to a close with a theological reflection. The groups continue to meet to plan their actions. The process that has been set in train much resembles the process of conscientization commended by Paulo Freire, involving the 'learner' becoming critically engaged in reviewing his or her world and experiences, challenging taken-for-granted ways of seeing and understanding, and resulting in an increased ability – and commitment – to transform reality.

Conclusion

The challenge in relation to apt liturgy is to recognize and then to have the confidence to seize the moment when it is an appropriate offering. This calls for sensitivity, creativity and pace – or else the moment will be lost. To achieve this means being immersed in the daily life of local communities in order to be aware of the undercurrents of feeling and concern and to be credible as someone (or representative of an agency) who can handle strong emotions. This calls for significant emotional literacy as well as courage.

Effective apt liturgy also calls for the ability to offer relevant concepts and symbols that enable participants to move beyond emotional reactions to a more reflective state. In offering symbols and stories that resonate with the circumstances, people are enabled to put their own experiences into a wider context, and from this a sense of solidarity is fostered – even with those who dwell on the other side of the globe. Finally, while the prompt for apt liturgy is often a sense of communal dismay, the aim of the liturgy is to enable people to move from despair towards hopefulness and re-engagement.

The process associated with apt liturgy is a distinctive, life-giving offering made by those who are confident in the incarnation of God and the eternal and universal nature of our life on earth. In a context where a sense of fragmentation and individualism dominates, the public offering of apt liturgy is indeed subversive, for it speaks of how we cannot live by bread alone.

Notes

1 The concept of apt liturgy was first developed by Ann Morisy, *Beyond the Good Samaritan*, London: Continuum, 1996, see Chapter 4, 'Praxis, power and liturgy in a secular world'. Morisy develops the concept further in *Journeying Out*, London: Continuum 2004, see Chapter 8, 'The foundational domain'.

2 *CULF in Plymouth Report*, 2005, section 7.2. Devonport Regeneration Company's Faith and Quality of Life Strategy.

3 *CULF in Plymouth Report*, section 7.4.

4 The prefix 'peri' is from the Greek. It means 'about', 'around' or 'beyond'. The rest of the word – 'cope' – is from the Greek *kope*, which means 'a cutting'. It is pronounced 'ko-pay'.

5 The term 'death before his eyes' was used by Boswell writing in his diary on having visited the philosopher David Hume. Boswell writes, 'I had a strong curiosity to be satisfied if he persisted in disbelieving a future state even when he had death before his eyes. I asked him if the thought of annihilation never gave him any uneasiness. Hume replied: "No more uneasiness than the thought that he had not existed before his birth".' Quoted in Michael Ignatieff, *The Needs of Strangers*, London: Hogarth Press, 1984, p. 83.

6 Abridged from <bbc.co.uk/history/historic_figures/unknown_warrior>.

7 *Beyond Our Tears* (London: CTBI, 2004), edited by Jean Mayland on behalf of Churches Together in Britain and Ireland, is a resource book for times of national tragedy and local grief – acknowledging that in such circumstances the right words can be hard to find.

8 John O'Donohue, 'Minding the threshold: towards a theory of priesthood in difficult times', in *The Furrow*, 49 (6); June 1998, pp. 323–35, p. 325.

9 Grace Davie, *Religion in Britain Since 1945: Believing Without Belonging*; Oxford: Blackwell, 1994.

10 In relation to apt liturgy, it is more appropriate to think in terms of participants rather than 'worshippers'. Worship is hard to achieve when the head is buzzing as to whether one has a faith or whether one really believes in the orthodoxies of a religion.

11 Paulo Freire, *Pedagogy of the Oppressed*, Harmondsworth: Penguin, 1972.

12 Morisy, *Journeying Out*.

13 Russ Parker, *Healing Wounded History*, London: Darton, Longman and Todd, 2001.

14 It is useful for others to know the terms of reference for CULF in Plymouth, given the scope for interfaith cooperation and practical application that the group achieved. The terms of reference for the group were to improve partnership working between faith communities and other organizations involved in regeneration and community development (CD); to develop an awareness of the resources and contributions faith communities can make to the experience of well-being in communities; to explore and demonstrate this in an 'event' aimed at improving effective and collaborative responses to those currently marginalized; and to encourage participation by members of faith communities in such events and a process that would maximize the likelihood of follow-up action. In the process of undertaking the above, information would be collated about the experience of faith group involvement in CD work in Plymouth which would build on a report (*Daily Service*, 2004) produced by Government Office South West in collaboration with the South West Council of Faiths on the contributions of faith communities to regeneration and the implications for enabling more faith group involvement in regeneration. The report on all this work, entitled *Walking the Talk: The Social Involvement of Plymouth Faith Groups*, was completed by Ann Jeffries for CULF by the initial June 2005 deadline. The most tangible outcome in Plymouth over subsequent months was the opening of a winter refuge for destitute asylum seekers. This has an inter-agency and interfaith steering group under the umbrella of Churches Together in Plymouth and is totally staffed by volunteers from churches across the city augmented by local students.

15 It is important to distinguish between apt liturgy and the far more rigorous process of healing wounded history. Apt liturgy acknowledges the

hurts of the past but is unlikely to have the scope to explore the dynamics in detail. Russ Parker's approach to healing wounded history enables people to engage with the distant past and not just events that belong to the recent past, or in Plymouth's experience, current issues.

16 Leonie Sandercock, *Mongrel Cities*, London: Continuum, 2003, p. 204.

6

Worship on Upper Street, Islington

GRAHAM KINGS

In the cosmopolitan context of Islington, how can an historic 'open evangelical' church provide worship that is authentic and connects with local people? We begin not in the church but on the streets:

> *Voice 1*: I don't think it right when there are kids round here . . . I dunno, I think it's a bit weird, I suppose, you know.
>
> *Voice 2*: I think it's good, because that's what Easter is about. I think they've done it well, in a modern way.
>
> *Voice 3*: Quite a shock. It's very powerful. Quite shocking as well.
>
> *Voice 4*: I think it brings it much more into the present.
>
> *Voice 5*: It's not what you expect to see when you're sitting outside eating breakfast.
>
> *Voice 6*: Oh, it's Christ, is it? We are wondering what it was all about. We weren't quite sure.

These reactions of various people, and other interviews, were recorded in Upper Street, Islington, London on Good Friday, 18 April 2003, and broadcast on the Easter Day *Sunday* programme of BBC Radio 4.[1]

Context

On hearing the word Islington, many people think of politicians and writers, restaurants and theatres. That may be true, and Upper Street – a mile long – has more restaurants than any other street in Europe. However, cheek by jowl with Georgian houses are housing estates that harbour multiple deprivation. The parish of St Mary's, Islington, includes the Town Hall, the N1 shopping centre, the Business Design Centre, the Almeida, the King's Head Pub and the Little Angel marionette theatres, but also various blocks of social housing and council flats.

According to Islington Council's statistics, in St Mary's ward, 47.4 per cent of residents still live in social housing; 17 per cent have a limiting and long-term illness, and 5.8 per cent are long-term unemployed. Drug and alcohol abuse as well as homelessness are also real problems in the ward as Upper Street has a significant street population. St Mary's is the 1358th most deprived ward out of 8414 across England and Wales.

St Mary's Church includes young and old, black and white, and rich and poor and is one of the few places that diverse groups of people can meet in Islington. 'Connecting people with God' is our mission statement, which we borrowed from Nokia and transformed with a couple of key words. Our mission in the community, focused on our Neighbourhood Centre and Crypt, includes a pre-school, open youth club, senior citizens clubs, assistance to the homeless, legal advice, and support for those suffering from addictions. We also have a church primary school, founded in 1710.

There has been a church on this site for nearly 1,000 years and there is a Norman stone, dated to between AD 1130–1150, in the crypt. The church itself has undergone death and resurrection, being the first London church to be bombed in the Second World War. The current building has the surviving 1754 tower, spire and crypt, and a 1956 nave and chancel, which from the outside matches the Georgian front, but inside is wonderfully spacious and light with no pillars, galleries or stained-glass windows.

Good Friday Procession, 2003

Tom Mannion, was carrying an 8-ft cross from the new N1 shopping centre to St Mary's Church in front of shoppers and the café society of Upper Street. He had recently played Mark Antony in the Royal Shakespeare Company's *Julius Caesar* and the neurosurgeon in the film *Iris* and is a sidesperson at St Mary's. About 500 people were following him in the procession. Some were passers-by caught up in the drama.

The idea began with a conversation over a lunch that I had with Shaun Lennard, the Roman Catholic priest at St John's Church, Duncan Terrace. Shaun reckoned that the 'halo' sculpture at the Upper Street entrance to the new shopping centre was not so much a 'halo' as a 'crown of thorns'. I agreed and suggested we needed to make that more obvious. How about an ecumenical procession on Good Friday? The sculpture is made of steel, and what looks like optic fibre cabling, wound round into a spiky wreath. It hangs high up, strung between the shops Next and Monsoon. The other matching sculpture, at the Liverpool Road entrance, is much larger and is of huge angel wings, stretching between Borders bookshop on one side, and the United Colors of Benetton on the other.

On Good Friday, Tom wandered into the Benetton shop and, in a changing room, put on a green robe and sandals and some fake blood make-up. He came out as Christ and quietly slipped into his place in the open area encircled by a large crowd, under the Angel sculpture. The band from the Anglican 'Church on the Corner' (a 'church plant' in a former pub) were singing, 'Were you there when they crucified my Lord?' Not everyone noticed Christ at first, for he arrived quietly. It was very moving to see a lonely, wretched figure, standing motionless with hands crossed at the wrists. I spoke briefly about what was going to happen and the significance of the sculptures.

Christ then shouldered the rough cross and set off through the crowd, which opened before him. He was accompanied by a funereal beat on an African drum and dancers from the group 'Icon', who are based in Cambridge and who portrayed the women of Jerusalem, wailing at the fate of Christ. Ali Eve, the leader of the group, had rehearsed local and Cambridge women in stark, vivid movements. Later she commented: 'What we were trying to express was the feelings and the emotions of the women who were gathered around the cross of Christ. We explored shock, paralysis and a despairing terror.'

Under the 'Crown of Thorns' sculpture, we stopped and Bernard Longley, the local Roman Catholic Bishop, gave a short meditation. As we moved on half a mile up Upper Street, passers-by joined us and people eating lunch at tables on the pavement were amazed. Jean-Luc Choplin, the head of Sadler's Wells Theatre, was part of the crowd that day. He had worked earlier in his career in a monastery in France. He commented: 'Wonderful. At the beginning of the twenty-first century, we are seeing something absolutely extraordinary. Artists are looking at invading public spaces to establish very strong links with the community in which they work.'

At the pedestrian crossing, I remember a black bus driver refusing to be waved on and holding up all the traffic for several minutes. At that stage the African drum mingled with the tolling of St Mary's tenor bell. Christ waited on the porch steps with a focused gaze, as photographers mingled around – appropriately, it seemed unseemly – and the crowd flowed into church. The organist, Andrew Adigun, was improvising some wailing-style music. Christ changed in a side room, and came out as Tom, who pinned the bloodied green robe to the cross as he carried it up the aisle, while the congregation sang, 'When I survey the wondrous cross.'

The cross was placed at the chancel steps and connected with the installation on the green chancel carpet. This had been created that morning by Miriam Kings, an art student at Central St Martin's College, London. It was the face of Christ, about 9 ft by 15 ft, made of women's clothes of varied colours, twigs and petals. She had run out of white clothes, and so used some Mission Praise books.

Janet Wootton, the minister of Union Chapel, the Congregational church in Upper Street, then invited the congregation to come up and bury the face of Christ under the Holy Communion table. To haunting piano music, Miriam led the people forward. Janet said: 'For me the significance is of being in solidarity with so many people in our troubled world, who are burying their loved ones. It also means that we die with Christ, as Christians, and we rise with him – so we're burying our sinful nature.'

This public evocation of the passion of Christ, using sculpture, drama, dance, music and art, was all over in one hour. Many people stayed for the following two hours of traditional 'meditations around the cross'. I was deeply moved by the whole procession, a condensed update of the medieval mystery plays in postmodern Islington. We were creating an event that demanded an explanation. When worship and the good news are presented imaginatively and evocatively and in a public place, then people do ask questions.

In particular, I felt it combined two key themes of St Paul's theology: the concept of 'Christ dying in my place' – he did that for me – was the focus of the walk up Upper Street, and the reality of 'being in Christ', which came alive for me with the burying of Christ – and our sins in him – under the Holy Table. I learnt later that the Orthodox Church have a rite involving a richly embroidered veil called the *epitaphion* (Greek for 'belonging to the burial'). This is carried in procession on Good Friday and later placed on the altar. Without realizing it, it may be that we were transposing an ancient ceremony into a new key.

On Easter Day, all that remained of the installation of the face of Christ under the Holy Table were two linen cloths. Ali Eve danced a poignant Mary Magdalene approaching the tomb and then being shocked by a man she thought was the gardener. The moment of recognition, as she heard her name 'Mary', was unforgettable.

For the sermon, I gathered the young people up into the chancel area, where Ali had just danced, and talked about the three 'words' the risen Christ said to Mary Magdalene: two questions and then her name. Just as the children were returning to their seats, Tom Mannion came up the chancel steps from the crypt, wearing a white robe. They were astonished and may well remember it for the rest of their lives. He showed the young people his hands and side and then repeated to them, and to the congregation, Christ's words to Mary: 'Why are you weeping?', 'Who are you looking for?', 'Mary'.

Unknown to us, a Canadian church historian, Alan Hayes, was in the congregation and he later wrote up his reflections.[2]

Good Friday Procession, 2004

The following year, we repeated the ecumenical procession but with some key differences. The cross was carried by Duane O'Garro, a young black student at the community Anna Scher theatre, who was also a street jazz dance teacher at our Youth Club.[3] It was just after the release of Mel Gibson's provocative film. In an interview with a local paper the week before, Duane said: 'I'm planning to see *The Passion of the Christ*, but am pleased that there will be no torture scenes in the N1 shopping centre. The cross is very heavy, but when Nick Adams, our senior youth leader, told me that the churches wanted me to carry it, I thought – yeah, let's go for it.' So, the passion of the Christ came to Upper Street – not with the gore and the blood, but with the staggering of a local youth leader.

Duane is more slightly built than Tom Mannion and he needed the help of a Simon of Cyrene figure. Tom mentored him, helped him get into role, clothed him in the same green robe as the previous year and put on his make-up. In front of the Business Design

Centre, half-way along the route, Christ collapsed under the weight of the cross. As arranged, another member of the youth club, a Muslim who was considering the impact of Christ on his own life, carried the cross. Muslims believe that Jesus was taken straight to paradise and did not in fact die on the cross, but someone replaced him at the last moment. Many Muslims believe that was Simon of Cyrene.

The sculpture in St Mary's that year had been brought over from the vicarage. It was 'The Eighth Hour', by Jonathan Clarke, who is based near Bury St Edmunds. Christ's body is of aluminium and his arms and legs are the wood of the cross.[4] Christ is not so much on the cross, as in the cross. The Cross is his body (cf. resonances with the medieval poem, 'The Dream of the Rood') and it seems to be taking him over, as he takes on the sin and evil of the world. There are echoes of Samson pushing the pillars of the temple. Judges 16.30 states: 'So those he killed at his death were more than those he had killed during his life.' Christ positively reverses that verdict. He *saved* more by his death than he had during his life.

Guy Laurence, Pastor of Cross Street Baptist Church, led a meditation and invited the people to come forward and pick up some dried petals and spices of pot-pourri and scatter them at the foot of the sculpture. Again, the whole event lasted only one hour and then moved into the four half-hours of hymns, reading, sermon, prayer and meditation. At ten to three, I invited all the congregation up to gather around the sculpture. What they did not know, was that the top – the figure of Christ and the arms of the cross – could be separated from the 5-ft-high wooden base. I invited an elderly white man, Tom Quantrill, and an elderly black man, Hugh Duesbury, to be Nicodemus and Joseph of Arimathea (John 19.38–42). They took off the top of the sculpture and buried Christ under the Holy Table. They then scattered more pot-pourri over Christ.[5]

On Easter Day, I took over to the church from the vicarage a painting called 'Rabbouni', by Silvia Dimitrova, and used it as a visual aid in the sermon. Silvia is a Bulgarian painter now based at Downside School, near Bath. I had seen her earlier work at the London Art Fair at the Business Design Centre in Upper Street. She paints both traditional Bulgarian icons and modern love paintings but until 'Rabbouni', had never painted a modern religious painting of love. In her exhibition in our Crypt Gallery the previous year, we highlighted a quotation by the Christian scholar of Islam, Kenneth Cragg: 'The sacred is the destiny of the secular and the secular is the raw material of the sacred.'

I had given Silvia the text of John 20.11–18 and had asked her to paint the face of Mary Magdalene at the moment she heard her name pronounced by the risen Christ. There seemed to be many paintings of the conversation a few seconds later, when Christ says, 'Do not cling on to me' (*Noli me tangere*), but I knew of none of the exact moment when her faith came alive, as she heard her name. When Silvia delivered the painting (egg tempera on wood), it included not just Mary, but Christ, the angels, the trees in the garden and a hint of the empty tomb (it may be seen at <www.stmaryislington.org>). I wrote the following poem while meditating on it:

> Who is this woman facing this man?
> Head lightly inclined,
> eyes wide open, gazing;
> hands uplifted, palms upward, surprised;
> gorgeously arrayed.
>
> Who is this man facing this woman?
> Coming from the right,
> profile clear, bearded;
> hand outstretched, palm down;
> gloriously apparelled.
>
> Behind her, two angels hover
> reflecting her shape:
> behind him, scented trees lean
> setting the scene:
> below her, a dark opening hints.
> All silent witnesses.
>
> The eyes have it:
> focus of tension and attention.
> One word awakes her: 'Mary'.
> One word responds: 'Rabbouni'.
>
> Their hands shape a triangle
> at the centre of meeting:
> her two, shocked and suppliant;
> his one, blessing, calming, sending.

Good Friday Procession, 2005

The following year Mark Shelton, the African-American former pastor of Union Chapel, Upper Street, carried the cross, wearing the same green robe. The drumming was much louder than previous years and was led by Bernie Gardner and Ed Nixon, from the group 'Heat Drummers', based at St Mary's, Bryanston Square, London. As Mark carried the cross up the central aisle, they continued their devastating, threatening drumming.

Shaun Lennard, a Roman Catholic priest, led the meditation. As the congregation had entered the church, they had each been given a drawing pin and a red ribbon. He invited them forward to pin their sins to the cross of Christ and leave them there.

Then Stephen Oliver (the Bishop of Stepney), Shaun and I lifted the top of the cross, now covered in ribbons, to connect with the bottom of the 'lectern' sculpture on the Holy Table, with the base of the cross still on the green chancel carpet.

This sculpture, 'Christ and the Children', is also by Jonathan Clarke. It is an aluminium 'lectern', made up of two parts, and its usual place is on the side aisle communion table in St Mary's. The cantilever design allows the 'lectern' to be adjusted, so that children can read at their level and adults at theirs. The reading plate is engraved with the name of Harvey Lewis, who died tragically aged only three months, and whose funeral I took in Lent 2003. It was commissioned in his memory by his parents, Karl Scott and Julie Lewis, who live on one of our local estates (it may be seen at <www.stmaryislington.org>).

The reading plate, behind, is attached to the figure of Christ, in front, and this whole piece can be lifted off the main base, on which there are figures of children in front of an elliptical background. At the lower level, for children, when looked at from the front, Christ is seen blessing the children. At the higher level, it transforms into the disciples watching the ascending Christ.

Bishop Stephen led the first of the four half-hour meditations and at ten to three, with the congregation gathered around, the lectern's reading plate and figure of Christ were buried under the Holy Table.

At the time of writing, plans for Good Friday 2006 include hanging a large representation of the 'curtain of the temple' (Mark 15.38 and Hebrews 10.19–21) between the main lectern and the pulpit, obscuring the Holy Table. The cross will be carried by Victor Virdi, who became a Christian on a recent Alpha course, and he will place it in front of the curtain. The cross will then suddenly crash into it, tearing it from top to bottom. This will be along a previously prepared tear, which will be taped up with Velcro – spontaneity has to be well prepared for . . . Then strips from the curtain will be ripped up and given to the people, as they come forward to wrap the 'body of the cross' with the material, and with pot-pourri, for burial (John 11.44 and John 20.6–7).

Guest Service and the South African Mysteries

In November 2002, I interviewed God at one of our Guest Services – well, at least an actor playing God. This was Vumile Nomanyama. He was part of the cast of *The Mysteries*, the spectacular South African update of the medieval Chester mystery plays. They played to packed houses at the Wilton Music Hall in the East End, near the Tower of London, and then later at the Queen's Theatre in the West End.[6]

Some of the cast were staying at the Royal Foundation of St Katharine, a retreat centre in the East End where I go for monthly quiet days. Ron Swan, the Master, put me in touch with their director, Mark Dornford-May. Mark kindly agreed that the cast would present some key scenes as part of a guest service at St Mary's and we agreed to provide a lunch for the cast in the crypt café.

Mark had gathered talented young South Africans from the townships and reworked the mystery plays with dance, song, and drumming into that context, using a mixture of languages: Zulu, Xhosa, Afrikaans, English and even some Latin. In the theatre, it was the most powerful presentation of the gospel I have ever seen. In church, it produced tears of worship and commitment in many people.

The vibrancy and energy of the story and of the cast were extraordinary. The context in South African townships was compelling – complete with Pilate as a white governor and black murders through 'necklacing' (setting fire to a tyre placed around the neck). The sheer range of the biblical story was breathtakingly portrayed. Noah's party after the flood was interrupted by the arrival of God: everyone froze, worried about celebrating too much. But God broke the tension by tapping the wine bottle he was carrying and joining in the party.

In particular, I enjoyed the sheer humanity of Jesus. He had difficulty learning a rhythmic hand slap 'code' from his mother but then used this to great effect in calling his disciples. When they were huddled in the upper room, after his crucifixion, they were not sure it was he who suddenly appeared. Then he performed the rhythmic slap again, slowly at first, which was picked up by his followers. Again after tragedy, recognition, joy and dance intermingle.

At the beginning, they had taught us the haunting theme song, which the young Jesus plays first on his tin whistle. At the end of the service, the cast surrounded the whole congregation and led us in singing the song of the resurrection. I have rarely been so caught up in worship.

Civic services and Muslim interviews

There are two metal brackets on the right front pew of St Mary's Church. They are for the Mayor's mace and the Mayor of Islington has a special seat in that pew. Of our recent civic services, two have been particularly significant.

In November 2001, after the Al Qaeda attacks of 9/11 in New York and Washington, we had a civic service of commemoration and Kristin Bruess, an American member of St Mary's, read out the list of nationalities of the people who had died in the World Trade Center. The service included an interview with Musa Admani, the imam 'chaplain' at London Metropolitan University. He was very perceptive and talked about his work with Muslim students, doing Koranic study with them. At that stage, Abu Hamza was still preaching at the radical Finsbury Park mosque, which is about 30 minutes' walk from here.

In November 2005, we had a celebration of International Islington, including another interview with Musa, who spoke about Muslim responses to the London bombings in July. A couple of months previously, he had led a discussion seminar in St Mary's on that subject and we were struck by how the present Islamic context was similar to pre-Reformation England. Musa is trying to encourage younger Muslim students to get to know the text of the Koran in English translations. A former student testified to becoming more moderate as a Muslim, once he had studied the text of the Koran, rather than relying on what he was told by his leaders the Koran said.

Also at that service, a 10-minute film was shown of the life of Samuel Ajayi Crowther, the first black African Bishop in the Anglican Communion. Crowther, a freed slave, had attended St Mary's Parochial School in 1826 and trained for ordination at the Church Missionary Society Institute on Upper Street in 1842–43. He was consecrated Bishop of the Niger in 1864. The producer of the film, Frank Macaulay, is the great-great-great-grandson of Crowther. In an interview during the service, he told of how he had found St Mary's through a web search for the name of Crowther, had then joined our Alpha course and had come to faith in Christ.

Christmas Day broadcast, 2004

BBC Radio 4 recorded their 2004 Christmas Day Service at St Mary's. Colin Morris, the Methodist broadcaster, preached. John Rutter directed the Southbank Sinfonia and Pegasus choir in a selection of his own Christmas compositions and arrangements of well-loved carols. Hannah Gordon, the actress, did the readings and the service was led by Bishop Stephen Oliver and me. Prayers were read by Barbara Quantrill (in her seventies), who runs our homelessness project and senior citizens club, Jemma Gilbert (in her twenties), who is our churchwarden, and Peter Oluyinka Scott-Odusola (under 10), who attends our school and Sunday school.

The following litany, which I had written for an evangelical Anglican conference in 1993, was used. Rehearsing the congregation was good fun for it goes to a regular beat, which is almost a rap rhythm. The impact of the phrase, 'And the Word became flesh', was emotive and emphatic. The penultimate two lines were divided between different halves of the congregation and the final line was proclaimed together.

In the beginning was the Word

God spoke his Word through
   Abraham and Moses,
   Deborah and Hannah,
Samuel and David,
Isaiah, Zechariah.
It is written   it is written.
And the Word   became   flesh.

God spoke his Word through
    Mary and Elizabeth,
    Simeon and Anna,
    Peter and Paul,
    Matthew and Johanna.
It is written   *it is written.*

God speaks his Word in
    Urdu and Tamil,
    Xhosa and Hausa,
    Spanish and English,
    Mandarin and Maori.
It is read   *it is read.*

In the beginning was the Word
And the Word became flesh.

It is written   *it is read;*
It is old   *it is new;*
It is God's   *it is true.*

Praise Nights

Our regular morning service is very popular and has an all-age orchestra on the first Sunday of the month, a band on the second and fourth Sundays, and a choir on the third (and fifth) Sundays. Last year, we planned to renew our evening worship. St Mary's ward has a very young age profile, with the majority of residents between the ages of 20 and 39. Many of these people are single, 54 per cent, with 44 per cent living alone. In response to this and to the buzz of Upper Street, in the autumn of 2005, we started 'Praise Night' services at 7.30 p.m., after our quieter evening service at 6 p.m. This is led by Dan Damon, a BBC World Service presenter, and is 'broadcast' (not too loudly) to Upper Street (taking further the idea of the Muslim 'call to prayer' . . .). Special lighting effects light up the church porch, and people walking along Upper Street can clearly see something is happening. Again, like the Good Friday services, an event is being created which raises questions and demands an interpretation.[7]

Dan runs the informal service like a radio programme, complete with praise songs from a girl band, interviews, readings and talks. I am usually outside on the pavement distributing leaflets, with some others, and encouraging people to drop in. A surprising number do – so far, about 18 passers-by on an average Sunday. It is rather like some Orthodox services where people can come and go. Some stay for five or ten minutes, others for 20 or 30 minutes and some for the whole hour.

Conclusion

Creating and sustaining worship that is welcoming to so many diverse groups are challenging and crucial. We have found that authentic worship is also powerfully evangelistic, for its truth and con-textual sensitivity have dynamic drawing power. At the end of our morning services, as the clergy and lay leaders process down the aisle during the last hymn, the congregation turn to face Upper Street, which they can see through the open west doors. With a sweep of the arm, the dismissal is given, sending God's people out into God's world to live and work to his praise and glory.

Notes

1 <www.bbc.co.uk/religion/realmedia/sunday/s20030420b.ram>
2 <http://individual.utoronto.ca./hayes/churchreviews/stmarys.htm>
3 <www.stmarysyouthclub.org.uk>
4 <www.martynmission.cam.ac.uk/Cross.htm>. See also Mission Theo-logical Advisory Group, *Transparencies: Pictures and Prayers for Mission and Reflection*, London: Church House Publishing, 2002, Chapter 4.
5 A photo montage of this and the 2003 procession, from the front cover of *The Reader*, Winter, 2004, may be seen on <www.stmaryislington.org>.
6 The DVD is available from Heritage Theatre video productions and the BBC.
7 A *Time Out* journalist wandered into our Praise Night service and wrote it up in the 'I love Sunday' edition. He wrote: 'Is God a DJ? Mixing hard Christianity and soft rock, the brand new Praise Night at St Mary's Church on Upper Street is the brainchild of Dan Damon (who you may know from *Religion* on the BBC World Service). Drinkers wandering by are tempted in by mobile disco lighting and Bible-stompin' rock spilling out into the street – inside, a small but enthusiastic congregation watches a live band from the pews.' (*Time Out*, 22–29 March 2006, p. 17)

Part 3

WINDOWS INTO OUR WORLD

7

A triangle of stories

MARK WATERS

Introduction

As human beings, we are constituted by the stories that we tell about ourselves. In order to be a person, I need a narrative that tells me who I am in relation to others, and gives me a sense of identity. It is this ability to be self-reflective and to weave the things that happen to us into narratives, or meaningful stories, which marks us out as a species. We are not always necessarily conscious of this process going on inside us but it will nevertheless be shaping all that we do or say, and will be giving us that sense of who we are and how we relate to our world.

We will shape and reshape such stories throughout our lives as our experiences and circumstances change. They will be particularly affected by the feedback we get from others as we relate to them, and also by the various crises, achievements, celebrations and milestones which living our lives brings.

Counsellors and therapists are very familiar with the stories we tell about ourselves. They have to listen over and over again to the many ways in which it is possible to end up with stories that hinder personal development and may drastically diminish a person's life. Such stories, arising perhaps from ill-treatment (or perceived ill-treatment) by others may lead us to write ourselves a script about being unworthy. Or, stories resulting from the effects of trauma may have left us fearful and unable to grasp life fully. Good therapists will also be able to tell of many instances in which people have been able to reach a position of telling themselves new, more appropriate stories which enabled them to function in a better way in their lives and to get a truer and stronger sense of self.

At the less vulnerable end of the human spectrum we know that individuals like Lance Armstrong, seven-times winner of the awesome cycling challenge Tour de France, and victor over cancer, will have a particularly robust narrative which informs the way in which they live their lives.

As we age, we hope that our narratives about ourselves may perhaps sit more comfortably with us and be less dramatically affected by outside events. We have all met older people whose serenity and gentle but firm sense of themselves have been an example of a life well lived and much enjoyed.

And we will all have encountered people who are unable or unwilling to change the story that they carry about themselves. People who are stuck in a particular narrative which is so obviously unhelpful for themselves, and for others who try and relate with them, resulting in a self-image which is rather like a stuck and scratchy record. Such individuals have, for some reason, been unable to successfully integrate their own story with the stories of others or the stories of their world. They have entered a self-referential closed circle.

Frederick Buechner in his book *Now and Then* explains why stories are important in understanding the life of faith:

> If God speaks to us at all other than through such official channels as the Bible and the Church then I think that he speaks to us largely through what happens to us . . . because the word that God speaks to us is always an incarnate word – a word spelled out to us not alphabetically, in syllables, but enigmatically, in events.[1]

At different points and places in our lives, these personal stories come into tension with other stories. In fact, it is only to the extent that we are able to integrate our own stories with other stories that we arrive at any sense of congruence as human beings. Our stories can never be little islands of personal identity but only make sense when connected to other narratives – both individual ones and the wider, more communal stories. In the end, the ways in which we are able and willing to change and develop our stories will tell the tale of our salvation, and the extent to which we are willing for our lives to be grounded in the love of God.

Worship through stories

Christian faith, and its expression in worship and final fulfilment in action, are an invitation to bring different sets of stories together. There are three sets of these stories, operating at different levels in our lives, which we need to connect to each other: stories about individuals, stories about communities and stories about God.

My story and your story

The first set of stories is about me (and everyone else gathered together here). We come in all our unique particularity to this public space set aside for the worship of God. Here in this space, if I allow it, my fragile ego can be safely unveiled. Here I may bring, and offer, the totality of my experience as an individual: my triumph and success in building my business; my struggles and delightful joys involved in sustaining meaningful and authentic relationships with my wife, children, friends and colleagues; my fear and sense of diminishment at contracting cancer; or the realities of living on this deprived estate.

To worship means to 'give worth'. But to give worth to God also demands that I come with some recognition of my value, my own uniqueness and preciousness before God, and an awareness of the things that I am either celebrating or struggling with at this moment in time. These things may not always be entirely clear, but it is at least important that I try and approach worship in a spirit of openness to what God may reveal to me through this corporate act in which I am participating with equally unique others. And part of my antennae must also recognize those others and the significance of this gathering together under God:

> My story is important not because it is mine, God knows, but because if I tell it anything like right, the chances are that you will recognise that in many ways it is also yours. Maybe nothing is more important than that we keep track, you and I, of these stories of who we are and where we have come from and the people we have met along the way because it is precisely through these stories in all their particularity . . . that God makes himself known to each of us most powerfully and personally.[2]

Shared stories

The second set of stories is about both the community I inhabit, and all the other sets of communities that touch me in this increasingly global world. I come as an English person living on Merseyside. I come as part of a militarily dominant, Western capitalist culture at the beginning of the twenty-first century of the Common Era. I come as a northerner in a socially and economically divided Britain. I come as both recipient and victim of the consumerism that brings me comfort and plenty, and yet which also threatens my existence on this over-populated and polluted planet. I come as a reader of this morning's news of the latest tsunami or the upturn in the Dow Jones index on the Stock Exchange. I am shaped by all of these stories, and so are you:

> The Exodus literature mounts an argument that individual person-hood is always a communal enterprise . . . the stages are never merely about interiority and yet are always about interaction in which the person is evoked, assaulted, and impinged upon in transformative ways, depending on the parties to the interaction. Such a view would correspond to the notion of covenant which many take to be the overriding metaphor of biblical faith.[3]

Sacred stories

The third set of stories with which I engage in worship are those from my religious tradition – the accumulated wisdom of Christian communities across time – hewn from attempts to articulate the reality of God for themselves in their day. These stories include the Scriptures and the creeds, the particular liturgical tradition of which I am a part, as well as the sacramental realities of baptism and Eucharist as they have been enacted and celebrated down the ages. Here in this act of worship I am invited into the adventures of faith of my brothers and sisters in Christ over two millennia, and also those of the Hebrew people before them whose faith birthed the Christ. I am offered the opportunity of participating in their struggles and of learning from their faithfulness.

I will know God to the extent that these sets of stories are allowed to be present, and in some sort of creative tension with each other, within the acts of worship of which I am a part. Does my experience of worship allow these stories to feed off each other, to challenge each other, and to be informed by one another in an ongoing conversation? If so, I am opened to the possibility of having my story rewritten, and its significance deepened as it becomes part of a story of salvation – those wide open spaces of freedom which the word means. Then I might come to know what I am called in the next moment in this life of mine because the result of stories in such radical and creative tension is practical theology in which praxis plays a central role:

> Praxis knowledge is central to people whose fundamental human vocation is to engage together in making the worlds in which they live ... The punch in practical theology comes in two places. The first is in the methodological conversation between interpretations of our faith and interpretations of our socio-cultural and socio-economic situation. Second, the conversation is sustained until the agenda becomes clear, until faith in dialogue with lived experience levies claims and we know the claims.[4]

Yet churches face some difficulties in the ways in which they use these stories. If worship is highly individualistic, and my own story and needs and desires dominate this process, I risk moving off down the road of the project-of-the-self: an introspective journey towards individualism which is so much a part of our times. This individualism is not just a secular phenomenon but can appear in religious form, often in terms of a highly exaggerated, literalistic sense of personal relationship with God which some people sometimes wrap around themselves.

If worship focuses on collective stories of culture, and stays largely with them, I may be tempted towards the heady, over-oxygenated air of narrow, partisan social activism. Many churches involved in regeneration initiatives risk simply engaging with the community part of the triangle of stories, neither connecting their work with the realities of individuals living in an area, nor steeping their work in the deeper stories of our religious heritage.

If for safety's sake, or simply through habit, Christian worship sticks with the stories of God within the blanket of my religious tradition, sure as sure I will be heading towards some sort of fundamentalism – a stale, closed circle of religion which feeds off itself. Fundamentalism is unresponsive to the realities of the world because it has created its own inner reality designed not to be breached. Thus, it becomes increasingly divorced from its context, and, thus separated, risks becoming demonic.

Yet when brought together in worship, and kept in creative tension, these stories bring the profound depth and balance which good liturgy requires. And thus rooted, worship will bring me the possibility of life – in all its fullness. Of course, this will not be an easy life, but a life born of struggle, wrought from wrestling with the living God. And through these stories touching each other in Christian worship I will be called to some serious challenges; but the worship of the local church will thus have bite, and it will connect more directly with all those who enter the doors of the church.

This sort of worship, rooted in a real world in which we encounter God, offers a cycle of recognition, articulation, and action that will issue in three things:

1 I will be enabled to see myself with some sort of clarity: to see myself as others see me, and as I am known by God, and thus to know myself. To see through my delusions, and thus freed, to be available again for action in the world.
2 I will be enabled to think critically: to be able to stand back and make judgements about this world. To understand the systems in which I am complicit. To celebrate what must be celebrated but to be under no illusions about the toxic nature of much of the human environment.
3 I will be prepared to be sent out (with you) to act prophetically: to be able to articulate what it is that will advance human flourishing; to discern what needs to be celebrated and what must be strenuously uncovered, challenged, and changed. In other words, to know something of God and his call.

Different points of creative tension in the liturgy

Despite the pre-ordered nature of most of our liturgy, there are some key moments when these three sets of stories can inform each other most directly.

The sermon

The first and most obvious of these is the sermon. I hasten to add that creative tension only happens if the preacher is attentive to these different sets of stories and is prepared to do considerable wrestling with each one. Sermons in which a scriptural hook is simply used in order to indulge prejudices or pre-formed agendas will not do. Nor will sermons that are about general moralizing or simply repeating biblical themes, nor those that are just 'churchy'. The sermon should be part of a specific conversation with the body of Christ in a particular place at a particular time and are cognition that God is speaking to us now and not only in the past. This calls for considerable preparation and prayerfulness in putting a sermon together, and a wrestling with the points at which the Scriptures meet the contingencies of our lives – where the 'eternal intersects with time'.

The intercessions

Intercessions are conducted in most churches with varying degrees of success. Sometimes they are overly formulaic simply relying upon the variant forms of words provided in formal service books. These so easily pass most of us by or invite us to a very general recognition of vague perceptions of our world. The other end of the extreme is a mawkishness which results from an over-emotional response to individual suffering or struggle and which assumes a particular outcome from God. Intercessions should be specific and concrete. They must not become second sermons, nor endless telling God what God is, or trying to second-guess a divine response. Instead they should give some sense of a genuine concern for specific and particular things. Intercessions should be genuinely humble: after all, they are about not-knowing; they represent concerns which are beyond our power to tackle or perhaps even beyond our ability to understand. They describe our human helplessness but within the very real hope that there will be some answer to our human concern.

The penitential rite

Too often, the penitential rite becomes either a tokenistic moment because it is taken too lightly and unspecifically, or it becomes an opportunity for an unspecified blaming about the awfulness of our human condition. Neither is appropriate.

The penitential rite is a crucial corporate act within the Eucharist. It asserts the basic Christian hope of the availability of forgiveness, an endless opportunity for recognizing our faults, turning in a new direction and starting again. It is not an invitation to morbidity or to false humility. Instead it asks of us a sense of reality and due proportion.

A major issue in thinking about the use of the penitential rite is its place within the order of the liturgy. It has become increasingly common to place the rite at the beginning of the liturgy as a sign of a humble approach to God that recognizes 'the sin which is ever before us'. There can be good reason for this usage, especially in a community that has a daily Eucharist. But from the very beginning of a ministry in one of the most deprived wards in the UK, I found myself in real difficulties with this practice. When a community is so ground down by generations of poverty, and when self-esteem and confidence are at such low levels, to make the rite of penitence the opening approach to God in the liturgy seems to me to be at least insensitive, and at worst sadistic (see also p. 136).

So it is a missed opportunity when the penitential rite and its introduction are formulaic, non-specific, and blunted by our familiarity with liturgical texts. Instead they should be crafted to become a key moment in the liturgy upon which the whole movement turns as fear and shame are transfigured into praise and thanksgiving through the forgiving, healing mercy of God.

Getting this right will involve worship leaders in carefully introducing the penitential rite with words which link it to what has gone before in the liturgy and particularly in the sermon and intercessions which should have incarnated the liturgy in the realities of people's lives. This of course is implying that the penitential rite should not be at the beginning of the liturgy as a basic approach to worshipping God but should come later on as a response to what has been heard in the Scriptures, interpreted for our day in the sermon, and raised as concern in the intercessions. The penitential rite should not be too individualistic. This is a time of corporate prayer; a chance to reflect upon the failure of our common life as much as our individual transgressions. We come before God at this point in the liturgy as representatives of the human family in full awareness of our ever-present propensity for evil and of a seemingly unending litany of horror stories of the violence and cruelty which human beings can inflict upon one another. We come in the knowledge that there is another way, and in strong hope that the light will not be extinguished by all the darkness. Thus, the penitential rite becomes a key part of our approach to communion, or even a condition of it. This hope is then liturgically acted out in the sharing of the peace in which we proclaim the sort of community we hope one day to become. Like the intercessions, the penitential rite should be surrounded with appropriate amounts of silence to convey something of the gravity of our concern and condition and a genuine willingness to open ourselves at points of considerable vulnerability and pain in searching for new and appropriate responses to real things happening in our world.

The opening prayer

Within the Anglican tradition, this prayer continues to be known as the 'collect' which implies the collecting together of the various themes of the day, whereas in the Roman tradition in its modern, simplified form the word 'prayer' is simply used. The opening prayer has been used in different ways in different traditions.

In more liturgical traditions, the collect acts as a gathering prayer for a particular Christian celebration, whereas the prayers commended and compiled by the International Commission on English Texts (ICET) relate the opening prayer to the themes in the three-year lectionary, in some cases, lifting phrases verbatim from the biblical texts for the day. In some churches in the past there was deemed to be a need to have the same prayer for particular Sundays and Feast days in order for people to be able to memorize the prayers and so give them some liturgical anchors. Today that need has largely disappeared partly due to changes in churchgoing patterns which mean that far more people attend every two or three weeks rather than weekly. Also the pace of liturgical change has meant that there is no longer for many people that sense that we are holding exactly the same service here in our church as all the other churches in our denomination. This frees up the opportunities provided by collects in various ways. First, it means that we can be freer and more independent about language. Many collects in the past have been archaic in style. But there is now a range of collects using different forms of language allowing collects to speak to different congregations and different occasions in new ways as well as old. Second, we have seen a huge widening of the imagery used in the writing of collects. Traditional collects employ metaphors for God that are often exclusively masculine and often associated with images of power and might. More recent collects have taken opportunity to employ a much wider range of images. They are often more intimate, use both masculine and feminine images, give a sense of the vulnerability of the Godhead which is always implicit in an incarnational theology and make use of a more direct style rather than the obfuscation which attended more traditional collects.

An alternative to using either traditional collects, or more modern ones, is to write your own in a style which suits your community. This means that collects can be clearly connected to the readings of the day, or the thoughts of the preacher, or both. This can give a much more cohesive and immediate sense to the liturgy.

The preface to the eucharistic prayer

As the liturgies of the Western tradition have been slowly re-forged in recent years, and as liturgy as a subject and a practice has developed and grown, we have been provided with a wealth of alternatives for this part of the liturgy, often most beautifully crafted. But I wonder if this is enough. The prefaces often begin 'And now we give you thanks because . . .', and go on to describe in different ways God's past work of incarnation. But if we really believe in incarnation we are not just talking about the past, we are talking crucially about now. Frederick Buechner comments again in *Telling Secrets*:

> God himself showed how crucial human life is by actually living one and hallowed human death by actually dying one and who lives and dies still with us and for us and in spite of us. I believe we are called to see that the day-to-day lives of all of us – the things that happened long ago, the things that happened only this morning – are also hallowed and crucial and part of a great drama in which souls are lost and souls are saved including our own.[5]

So there is a strong case for an extempore preface at this central point of the liturgy concluding what the specially crafted collect has initiated and anticipated – some expression of what we believe God is doing now, in us and through us and our community of faith. After all, was it not that great liturgist, Hippolytus, who set us the first example of this practice? He was a third-century bishop whose handwritten eucharistic liturgy still exists in a fragmentary form. Its eucharistic prayer has formed the model of much recent liturgical revision but it did not have a formal preface. It simply said that the Bishop may pray providing it is orthodox.

Baptism

In Anglican churches, and others which advocate infant baptism, there is sometimes a difficult tension to be held between wanting to be welcoming and accepting of local families and their newly born children, and the need for baptism to be a meaningful event which signals some real sense of spiritual commitment rather than a chance to get dressed up and have baby 'done' before the booze-up. Churches will differ in the ways in which they handle this tension. Some will refuse to baptise an infant until parents have attended a certain number of Sunday services. At the other end of a long spectrum, other churches will always agree to a request for the baptism of a child, placing their hope in the power of the grace of God to touch people's lives, and perhaps hoping that a service conducted with warmth, dignity and real humanity will in some real way engage with the baptism family. Working with the triangulation of stories can help in this dilemma and sharpen the impact of the liturgy of baptism.

In baptism, the individual story brought to the liturgy is of course the reality of this newborn infant in all its vulnerability, and with the huge helping of hope which at every baptism is offered for a child's future. The stories from the tradition we can pick and mix depending on what is going on at the moment. But the stories of community – the context in which this child will grow up – can provide a powerful way of engaging the baptism party in thinking about something beyond the 'warm fuzz' of the occasion.

The baptism of infants in the context of urban priority areas provides particularly sharp instances of why the social context is important to a life of faith. I usually 'borrow' the baby from the parents during my address at baptisms and hold the child as I talk about everyone's hope for him or her as they grow up. Everyone at the baptism will in one way or another have a hand in the upbringing of this little baby and could, depending on their response and relationship they have with the child or family, make a real difference to its life. In urban priority areas, I am always painfully aware of some of the realities of growing up in such an area. Statistically this little child is hugely more likely to get run down by a car in such an area or to suffer as a result of a whole range of accidents. Its health is more likely to be impaired, it can expect to achieve less at school, have more likelihood of being unemployed, and so on. The list is quite long. I find that people are often stunned to find out that this is the case, and to suddenly be aware of some of the realities of British urban life.

Without bombarding people with miserable statistics, I think it is a valid and effective practice to tell some of those stories of community, perhaps by using lay people to describe how the church is working in community initiatives to redress those imbalances and inequalities and how this is perhaps what it might mean to be drowned in Christ. It can be the beginning of people coming to see liturgy as something which is directly relevant to, and connected to the lives that they lead.

Ordination

Like most ordained clergy I return to the ordinal periodically, particularly at times when I am renewing or reflecting upon my vocation. I find interesting the shift in wording and emphasis that distinguishes the *Common Worship* rite of the Ordination of Priests from the Ordering of Priests in the Book of Common Prayer. The earlier rite exhorts clergy 'to seek for Christ's sheep that are dispersed abroad, and for his children who are in the midst of this naughty world, that they might be saved through Christ for ever'. At the beginning of the twenty-first century, the *Alternative Service Book 1980* Ordinal was still in force and said: 'He [*sic*] must set the Good Shepherd always before him as the pattern of his calling, caring for the people committed to his charge, and joining with them in a common witness to the world.' There is a discernible shift from the idea of rescue *from* a fallen world to one of mission *to* a world which is no longer described in any pejorative sense.[6]

The rite of ordination is of course conducted within every conceivable community, and it would be inadvisable and inappropriate to try to rewrite the ordinal for particular circumstances. But it would be good to think that one day we might have a proper preface for ordination, written by local people, which could spell out something more of the context of a new ministry, particularly in view of the growing practice of the ordination of priests to be conducted in the parish in which they are serving. This could be a wonderful opportunity for key members of the lay team in a parish, along with the clergy, to say something public and powerful about the situation in which they find themselves and in which they share a ministry. Such a shift could open the way for some of the community 'stories' with which it will be so important for a new priest to be engaged. It would also help to radically shift the focus of the ordination service from the role of the individual to that of the priest's role within the community of faith.

Here is a short personal anecdote showing faith in action:

Unity Baptist Church was a dirty, grey concrete building which stood next to a busy flyover in downtown New Orleans. At nine o'clock on a Sunday morning about six hundred people gathered every week. The congregation was almost entirely black.

The service began with a huge choir at the front leading spirituals with endless surging choruses which bring everyone to their feet. The altar party enters, led by 12 women dressed in long, white flowing robes, who sway and dance up the centre aisle as the choir continues singing. The pastors and deacons, men and women, follow. It takes about 15 minutes to get to the altar.

The heart of this liturgy is the stories that people tell within it about the lives that they lead. Stories of what it means to be black and poor in modern urban America which are seamlessly interwoven with the scriptural readings and the theology of the sermon. This congregation has a particular story as a people based upon their experience on the edges of this hugely affluent society. They know what it is to live in exile and in this liturgy they recall an earlier exile when their ancestors were exiled from their African homeland. Their faith is not an abstraction. This congregation knows that the Bible talks about the things that go on every day for the oppressed and downtrodden, and of a God who loves them with a huge heart. So, what the city leaders were doing or not doing about racism and racial violence in the city, and what was happening to the chances of black people getting decent jobs or decent houses was as much the story of the liturgy as the readings from the scriptures.

When the intercessions begin, six hundred people leave their seats and move forward to surround the altar, each with a hand on the shoulder of the person in front of them. And then the prayers begin, and you could not be in any shadow of a doubt that these prayers are meant.

After the service, one of the older women came up to me and spoke to me about her faith. 'I used to think I came from slavery,' she said, 'but the pastor has opened the book for me, and now I know that I come from royalty.'

Putting ideas into practice

To create worship events which bring together the different sets of stories that I have described requires careful preparation involving a group of people in a church. It cannot be done by pastor or priest alone. The heart of the preparation will be to practise telling our stories, and also the art of drawing out other people's life experience. People in church congregations often mistakenly believe that they know each other, but more usually they know each other only in a fairly superficial way (as in most human communities). First of all, a worshipping community needs to be agreed that all three of these elements – my story, our story, God's story – are crucial to coming to a knowledge of the Lord.

One suggestion as to how this might be done would be to identify a particular Sunday as an agreed date when we want to teach, through experience and through doing, that our worship involves these three aspects. Once agreed, three groups of people need to be identified to do some preparatory work. The first group with responsibility for 'my story' will be a group with pastoral concern and responsibility in the church; the second looking at 'our story' will be a group concerned with mission in its widest sense; the third will be concerned with our religious tradition. Most churches or parishes will be able to identify individuals who will have particular skills and sympathies to bring to such a division of church labour.

Each group will need a session to work separately on its particular brief. The pastoral group will spend prayerful time considering some of the individual needs of members of the congregation. This will not simply be a matter of being aware of those who are sick or in particular pastoral need, but will be more about thinking about the lives that people lead, the jobs they do (or do not do or have), and the particular insights and issues they might have as a result of this experience.

The mission group will be thinking in a wider context. It will be reflecting upon the patterns of influence which go to characterize an area, for example, government policies which affect people's lives; regional trends; crime levels; people's feelings about their neighbourhood; plans for development; local infrastructure, and so on.

The group reflecting from the perspective of our religious tradition will first look at the readings set for the day, doing some detailed exegesis of the texts in their group, bringing insights from their own lives which might echo things found in the Scriptures.

The next step is for the three groups to come together and share. What are individuals struggling with in the area? How much is this reflected in wider patterns of common life? What might God be saying to us about these issues through his word in Scripture? What resonances are set up across these sets of stories? What further thinking might be done as a result? Who might we need to talk to who might help us deepen our perspective on issues raised? What other pieces of Scripture might we want to study? How does this lead us into prayer?

The final step is to try to express whatever is being discovered or learned in a bold act of worship involving our hearts and minds. Perhaps this can be passed to a new group. Perhaps a small group drawn from each of the first three. Or perhaps everyone already involved can have a role in putting this service together.

I know that people will be saying that this is a lot of work – and it is. But this sort of exercise only needs to be done once for it to become a memory of the heart. Once taught this approach to stories and worship will have found a place in the community of faith and will only have to be repeated occasionally for it to be naturally a part of the worship people offer.

Conclusion

The three sets of stories with which we began this piece are more than just a device for organizing worship. Prayerfully kept in tension they invite us into a deeper reality – that of the Trinity. The ancient stories and sacred assertions of the Hebrew and Christian traditions represent the fatherhood of God. They affirm for us the givenness of creation and the acts of divine love that birthed the Christ in history.

In our own story we are called by Jesus, brother and friend, to understand our identities as rooted in God even in the middle of all of the mundane yet terrifying realities and choices of our own lives and the process of our becoming.

In the swirling, dynamic stories of the reality of life within the human community we enter the realm of the Spirit with all the possibilities which arise from risking diversity (and refusing Babel) in community.

And if we listen we will hear the Spirit calling; and if we are prepared to risk intimacy, we will feel her touch of affirming love, welcoming us into the real and fleshly communion of the Body of Christ.

Notes

1 Frederick Buechner, *Now and Then*, San Francisco: Harper, 1991.
2 Frederick Buechner, *Telling Secrets*, San Francisco: Harper, 1992, p. 30.
3 Walter Brueggemann, *Hope Within History*, Louisville, Ky.: Westminster John Knox Press, 1986, pp. 9–10.
4 Bernard Lee, *The Future Church of 140 BCE: A Hidden Revolution*, New York: Crossroad Publishing, 1959.
5 Buechner, *Telling Secrets*.
6 *Alternative Service Book 1980*, London: Hodder & Stoughton, 1980, p. 356.

8

Urban worship: rooted in reality, routed through the people

ERICA DUNMOW

Introduction

A famous liturgical writer, Prosper of Aquitaine, once wrote that our beliefs are revealed in our worship. Methodism's approach (which is my original setting) is often stereotyped as 'singing our theology'. Set forms of liturgy often say a great deal concerning what we believe about the transcendent God. But what about the immanent one? And what volumes do they imply about the incarnate, motley body of Christ gathered largely passively in a possibly tatty building on a cold, wet day? How are our lives in which we attempt to incarnate our understanding of Jesus' mission, reflected in the process of our worship?

In many churches of all denominations, little or nothing is done to value our realities, except maybe in the sermon and possibly the intercessions. And much is done to devalue them as we listen to the professionals leading us through someone else's understanding of God. Some might wish to do a hatchet job on the riches of formal liturgy, but that undervalues the spirituality that it communicates. However, we miss on a very important element of worship if we do not also develop our small 'c' charismatic ability to trust the Holy Spirit moving in our midst to shape our worship. This does not necessarily mean abandoning traditional prayers and music for we need to remain connected to the church universal. Nor is it unplanned chaos, and we must not confuse seriousness or dignity with solemnity, as informality is not the same as lackadaisicality. It is about bringing ordinary life into the presence of God to transform and empower those that live it. It is a plea for rooted worship routed through the people.

In urban congregations the gritty reality of life is often nearer the surface than in suburban ones, and it sometimes literally breaks in as stones through our stained glass or the random incursions into our buildings of local children, or street sleepers wanting a warm, dry place. Unless our worship connects with and addresses those realities, how can we expect people to understand how God interconnects with their lives and becomes more than a pietistic comfort blanket? Only when it does connect can the power of the incarnate God be seen not just in the mess of first-century Palestine but in the mess of twenty-first-century urban Britain. And when God becomes truly incarnate, the people who worship can more truly feel themselves beloved children of God, able and worthy to exercise God's mission. By saying that liturgy does not always have to be pretty and perfect and allowing the messiness of the ordinary into our worship, we are saying something about trusting that God is not as frightened and disempowered as we are by the unpalatable realities of life. A greater trust in God and themselves as beloved helps people move from dependence to action both within the worshipping life of the church and in its involvement in the wider community. Where that community life is consciously present in the worship, so there is a powerful integration between informed prayer and prayerful action. This is a key element in spiritual and economic regeneration. Without the former, all the financial resourcing and physical rebuilding of a community will not last and the underlying malaise will reassert itself as soon as the paint is dry. Even secular planners are beginning to talk in spiritual terms about what makes a good city for all its people.[1] As Prosper of Aquitaine knew, being more actively engaged in worship means enacting one's faith – which consolidates it more than simply saying words, and belief is strengthened. This gives people greater heart. It becomes clearer that faith is for '24:7' not just an hour on Sunday, and helps discern how to work with the Spirit in engaging in secular matters to bring the Kingdom nearer. The mission of the church becomes richer, less clergy-dependent and more routed through the people. It also becomes more relevant to people not part of the worshipping community. Some will be attracted by this active involvement in the wider community to encounter God.[2] Others will simply find God more accessible, as many of the newer 'house churches' and fresh expressions have already realized.

I will attempt to show how we might enable this enrichment of worship to become a powerful spiritual generator for our communities: first, through theoretical input, then some 'Here's some I prepared earlier' examples, more theory about sacraments, input about the role of the person in leading worship, and developing worship, and, finally, more practical ideas about the process of making change.

The liturgical traditions, where the words said and the actions performed are set by the denomination at a distance, can find it hardest to contextualize their liturgy, and, to be fair, they overcome this by spending time teaching catechumenates (to use their technical term for seekers) the meaning of and how to use liturgy as the foundation of their personal prayer. The set words then become the platform for people's own devotions – they learn how to make sense of and embed the fixed forms in their lives. But this is an entirely personal process – the local gathered body cannot communally express anything about its shared living before God. It is that communal sharing which helps to root the worship in local reality and which I want to encourage readers to develop. John Vincent's contribution to this book gives an analysis of how much more difficult this can be in churches where worship is predominantly sacramental and requiring authorized or ordained ministers, but I would still encourage people within those traditions to explore the flexibility that is there outside the Mass. The section on metaphorical sacraments may be interesting in this respect.

Worship rooted in urban settings

Ideally, in worship we are fully present as the people we are: in true humility aware of both our continued failings and our infinite worth in the eyes of our loving God. Unless we can be ourselves in church, we cannot fully worship – unless our lives are reflected within it we are segregating our faith from all creation. So often, even if real life does get a mention in our worship, it is as things we confess or make intercession for rather than celebrate. Placing the reality of people's lives in the context of worship endorses its validation by God. It can be a prophetic witness, against a counter-view centred on God's justice and love, to reflect in worship the experiences of people whose lives affluent people often dismiss as relatively valueless. Ann Jeffries and Ann Morisy take this further and show how worship conducted outside the church and its normal services completes the sense of living worship. I want to confine myself to what can be done in the normal Sunday service for two reasons. First, unless the worship in church is rooted and connected to people's ordinary lives, then the unchurched people who may be sufficiently excited by the relevance of extraordinary worship to venture into Sunday service will feel completely baffled and excluded (see the example from Gateshead below). Second, although there are many resources for more creative worship,[3] there are less about how it is developed. This is a sad lack as change is not easy to bring about in a way that is really inclusive, and a surprising number of church leaders feel frustrated by their lack of process skills in their wish to move things forward.

The fact that those in urban settings are often more sharply aware of pain in their lives means that worship in the positive mode alone denies a huge part of their reality. Kathy Galloway powerfully illustrates the place of the lamenting (as well as the praising) psalmody; I want to examine the way in which we enable people's lives to be fully reflected in our worship using an increasingly radical set of examples. In the course of this, I will touch on the role and skills demanded of the people leading worship to let this come about and a little of the process by which a reluctant congregation can be brought to accept this strange-seeming idea of celebrating their lives. None of this is unique to urban congregations, but because of their powerlessness, placing their lives in the centre of worship and involving them in the creation of worship is a deeply transforming prophetic act.

Sometimes even before people are ready to accept the messiness of their lives in worship they need to be made more sharply aware of the messiness of many Bible stories:

> I sat in on a Bible study at an inner-city Black majority Methodist congregation. The Black minister was leading it on Psalm 137, which is expurgated in the Psalms used for public reading at the back of the Methodist Hymn Book. He invited the group to read a verse each around the circle. The seventh reader hesitated at the awful words in front of her. 'Go on,' urged the minister, 'It's there in the Bible'. Stumbling over the unpalatable sentiments, the Afro-Caribbean pensioner finished the harsh text. There was an awkward silence, and then

the minister led the group into an initially hesitant exploration of their anger at incidents in their life. He was able to illustrate the importance of voicing anger to God as a way of avoiding sinful action towards those who sin against us.

Also, the huge variety of life experiences present in most urban congregations gives a much richer seam for resourcing worship – there may be real (ex-)prisoners and 'aliens' present as readings about them are read: 'I remember the sharp resonance the story of Ruth had when an exiled South African's voice cracked with emotion as she read the verse "And my people will be your people, and my God your God".' This is real liturgy, growing out of real lives and saying to those that live them – God is here with us.

Stages of engagement

In these practical sections we will start from examples that can be used in the most traditional liturgical patterns. We will then move in stages to some more informal types of worship interspersed with real examples.

Referring to local life

One of the simplest starting points is to exercise caution over language and illustration when leading worship. I never ceased to be irritated when leading worship in areas of low employment with the prayers issued for Unemployment Sunday that always referred to those without work as 'them'. Shifting our vocabulary from 'the poor' and 'the lonely' to 'people in poverty' and 'people who feel lonely' helps to establish their personhood separate from their (hopefully) temporary condition, and allows people to identify with those states as ones they may be in:

An experimental service that ran in a Methodist church in Durham for a couple of years used very low-tech methods of making prayer come alive. Two homeless people who'd become part of the congregation (initially because breakfast followed the formal part of the worship) helped to plan a service. That morning, intercessory prayer 'for outsiders' made a huge impact as the two street sleepers sat facing the walls outside the rest of the group.

This enabled our prayers, in Martin Wallace's phrase, to become more 'earthed'.

Sermon illustrations that value and commend the behaviour of, for example, lone parents relating well to their children or benefit claimants as valued carers rather than just receiving support, can simply and effectively begin to validate ordinary and often criticized types of people. Also, in our intercessions, do we ever pray for hospital cleaners and school caretakers as well as doctors and teachers?

Imaginative use of space and spaces

Action and sign can be interpolated into set liturgy to make it come alive:

> An estate church in Sheffield[4] took over a disused pub and was distressed that the level of break-ins meant that they needed to install shutters on the windows. This was in some way redeemed when the vicar decided to start the Easter service in 2005 with the shutters closed and the space lit only by candles. As they came to the point in the service where Christ's resurrection was proclaimed, the shutters rolled open, letting the light and view of the surrounding estate enter the space.

And how about occasionally celebrating communion in the context of a real meal, sitting around a real table, perhaps even a round one? Maundy Thursday is often a good excuse for this.

Coming forward to light a candle or place a symbolic object before a cross can give a non-verbal opportunity for engagement if lack of pews and other blocks to mobility make this feasible and is a valid technique in many settings (see also below the use of objects passed around).

Textual additions are also possible. In medieval times, musical embellishments of 'amens' became pieces in their own right, written in to the gaps in the set text. This can still be done in some traditions.

Hearing local voices

The next stage is to enable people's own voices to be heard before God. This starts with having rotas for Bible reading and intercessory prayer but can build beyond that:

I was recently conducting a service in an estate church where a loved minister who they knew as 'one of themselves' had been suddenly removed from ministry. They needed and wanted me to pray for him, but I didn't know him all that well, so I felt it was important that they could express their own thanks for his ministry or anger or grief at his departure. They were a small group, and so I offered a time of open prayer during which a lighted candle in a bowl and a tangle of lengths of dull coloured wool were passed round the seated group whilst the Taizé chant, 'O Lord, hear my prayer', played quietly. As each person received the bowl, they could if they wished pray a prayer of thanks out loud; as they were passed the wool, they could pray their distress. I had also made it clear that even if they didn't voice their prayer aloud the group would be praying with them as they held the objects. Some chose to quietly say a few words; others were silent, a few prayed loud enough for the whole group to hear. One long-standing member, who did not usually pray aloud, was able almost to unravel the wool as it came to him: he felt able to pray prophetically that the congregation would find a way through.

Used fairly frequently, this technique enables people to become more confident in voicing their own prayers in a public way. The use of objects passed round gives rhythm which avoids people wondering when to speak and validates those who remain silent as still having prayed and been prayed with. It also avoids the need for people with limited mobility, or stuck in pews, from having to leave their seats to place an object at a central point.

The Durham experimental service mentioned above sometimes used different 'stations' around the room where people could pray in different ways with practical actions and signs to engage with: a world map with flags to mark the place of a prayer request; a place just to sit and watch a candle; a sheet with the names of all sorts of people who might be seen working on a side street during a 24-hr period (e.g. cleansing operatives, district nurse, postperson, gas fitter, lollipop person, telecom engineer, paper delivery person, etc.); the words of the Lord's Prayer placed at intervals round a route to walk along.

This kind of provision for 'DIY liturgy' is increasingly being offered in church spaces that are open to the public. The Lightship 2000 run by the ecumenical chaplaincy to Cardiff Bay, has three such 'stations' in its chapel, with very simple suggestions of how to use the resource and short prayers on cards that can be said or taken away.

The Word from the people

The next stage is to entrust the Word to the people. This might take the form of a led discussion, or breaking into 'buzz' groups to discuss an aspect of the service, or simple, open reflection on the reading:

> The enriching impact of this technique was felt by several of the contributors to this book at the simple Eucharist we shared at a planning meeting. The person leading the worship simply commented after the reading of the set passage that they found it a hard one. This opened a space for some relatively honest sharing of the issue it provoked which deepened our sense of fellowship and connectedness with each other and God. For me, that made the healing reconciliation of the sharing of Christ's body, with the gathered body of Christ more palpably felt than normal. By allowing our own reactions to the Word, it had become more powerfully ours.

Some will recoil from the risk of unorthodox interpretations, but the use of a simple prayer asking the Holy Spirit to guide our thoughts and understanding can be helpful, as can the setting of some parameters to avoid argument. (The best and easiest is adhering to the Quaker-like convention of hearing each other but not replying.) Also there is a big difference in the level of authority claimed between saying 'I react in this way and think this' and saying that 'this is the received wisdom of the church' about the text. People are more adept at appreciating that difference than we often allow. The authorized worship leader might offer some final thoughts to give the 'orthodox' its place, or just join in. Again, sitting in a group facing each other helps create the atmosphere of shared reflection rather than authoritative teaching. This process feeds into and from lively Bible study techniques. Beyond worship, it can encourage people otherwise resistant to this, to use the Bible for private reflection as they learn to hear God talking to them directly from the text rather than just via the preacher: they are beginning to be empowered as theologians.

The Word in life

A further stage is using people's lives as sources of conversation with Bible stories. There is a current trend in ministerial training to encourage what is variously called practical, contextual or reflective theology, where real life, usually pastoral, issues that present us with challenges as to the relevance of our faith are reflected on in the 'Pastoral Cycle':

> A nurse from Liverpool looked at our understanding of life after death provoked by the release of children's body parts by Alder Hey Hospital. What is the appropriate liturgy to bury the organ of a child whose funeral has already taken place when this might be the second organ released? And how does it impact on our understanding of the resurrection body?

A church I attended in the East End of London was blessed with a very creative minister in the 1980s who used many different techniques to bring the weekday lives of the congregation into worship through this sort of process:

> A Lent series took the themes of the Sundays given in the Lectionary and then asked the permission of congregation members to use parts of their lives that illustrated those themes alongside the lectionary readings. They were written up in the simple service sheets and in several cases the person recounted their story as part of the 'ministry of the Word'.

In contrast to Kathy Galloway's example of the pit village where the minister ignored the miners' strike, this same east London congregation were highly politicized and regularly sent gifts of food and money to Houghton Main Miners' Wives Support Group:

> One memorable Sunday alongside the gospel – a passage about being a good neighbour – we had two modern 'epistles' read out: one a letter of thanks and news from the miners' wives, the other a letter of greeting, prayers and good wishes from a Black member who'd retired to Jamaica. They said all that needed to be said about the gospel.

Planning together

The next stage in developing rooted liturgy is that of involving a wider range of people in the putting together of the services. The east London church had three worship leaders, two lay and one ordained, and although we ensured maximum participation by the congregation – a lad with Down's syndrome often led the peace – it was planned by that team of three. John Vincent and Mark Waters have fine examples of liturgies developed by groups of people – but often these have been in the context of more informal, house-based worship. The next section examines how to translate this into more formal public worship.

Metaphorical sacraments

Metaphorical sacraments is a term coined for the continuum between real-life events and traditional sacraments. It aims to help make connections between the ordinary and the sacraments and to demystify the latter, based on an understanding of the spiritual processes embedded in them. I developed this term when exploring with Methodist deacons and presbyters how important sacraments were in their ministry. It is an identification of the praxis I had adopted when conducting worship in an ecumenical setting where not all could receive communion. We developed a pattern of agape sharings of tea and cake. We were clear this was not communion – the words and actions were different – but it had a deliberate, commemorative echo of Eucharist.

By extension, the offering of the hospitality of food can be seen as part of this continuum. In the same way, the setting up of a new community project can be said to be paralleling a human birth and if the project is dedicated to God in a service, isn't that even more like baptism? And if a new partnership comes into being – might a special service for that not be like a wedding? And if people are led through a liturgy of letting go and becoming reconciled to old hurts or anger, surely absolution and forgiveness are part of that? All these parallels can be extended away from worship but still have a metaphorical echo of a sacrament and an understanding of metaphorical sacrament will help in the shaping of 'apt liturgy', as explored by Ann Jeffries and Ann Morisy. During the research, once explained, with the caveat that Methodism actually only recognizes two sacraments, both presbyters and deacons could see their ministry as having links in this way. This was helpful especially to those deacons (who are, in Methodism, a permanent order ordained but not to the sacramental ministry) with a fairly 'high' approach to sacrament. Catholics may wish to explore these ideas as a way of enabling greater lay leadership in worship.

As stated above, Eucharist can be seen both as a subversive and an aggregating activity. Non-eucharistic worship needs to be shaped carefully so that it can evoke a similar sense of a journey travelled. Increasingly as lay leadership of worship becomes more common in many traditions, there is a danger that this sense of journey will be missing, but lay people can lead a metaphorical sacrament. Creating liturgy which is metaphorically sacramental can be very helpful also in youth groups who often wish to share together more deeply than just in prayer and song, but don't want the minister to have to come in to 'do' communion for them. This concept can also be useful in introducing unchurched people by stages to sacramental worship by helping them see the performative continuities more clearly between real-life events and sacraments. It also helps to avoid misunderstandings of the sacraments:

> I have seen completely unchurched young people totally freeze at hearing an invitation to come and drink Christ's blood, even though they were invited also to come forward for a blessing if they did not want to receive. They had no understanding of the picture-language, let alone transubstantiation, and that it wasn't real blood.

Creative and lay-led worship within this metaphorical framework is better rooted into the church's liturgical vocabulary and can draw upon and express a much greater variety of emotional and spiritual modes.

The ordained person's role in leading worship

As the liturgy becomes more rooted, emergent and communally planned, the role of the ordained person shifts a great deal. This is most difficult in those denominations where there is no tradition of lay leadership. Even where there is, clergy are not always willing to engage in, and are very seldom trained for, the sort of group planning processes that are required. If there are lay people with these skills, it might be best to let them facilitate the group process, and for the clergy to provide the liturgical and theological underpinning. When imagination and creativity do begin to flow – and in some groups it will take off – the clergy person may need to keep a necessary undercurrent of theological orthodoxy by occasionally asking, for example, 'What does this say about God?' or 'How does this reflect what we understand about God?' or 'What do we think God thinks about this?' Creative praxis should illuminate our eternal understanding of these matters, not mask it.

The freer the liturgy is from the set text, therefore, the more the responsibility for its orthodoxy and quality lies with the minister. This acquires much more understanding of the processes behind the format of liturgy. This can lead to the sort of questions raised by Tim Stratford, who, while adhering to formal liturgy, wants it to make more spiritual sense as a journey.

Many anthropologists have looked at the issue of the emotional power in ritual, of which Christian worship is a subset, and how this needs to be differentiated between power as 'force or control' and power as 'energy and capacity'. Without this, the emotional content can be manipulative. This brings into question both the ethics and the need for the 'officiants' of a ritual to create a particular emotional atmosphere. How far does the power then lie with them, as opposed to the collective flow of the Holy Spirit within them and all the gathered participants?

> Some research I undertook on the issue of power in worship sheds some light on this. I surveyed three congregations (Roman Catholic, Methodist and Assemblies of God Pentecostal) in a relatively economically disadvantaged suburb of an industrial town in Teesside.
>
> Respondents recorded that during a (eucharistic) church service their greatest points of contact with God were: (ranked first equal) praying led by the minister, reflection, and receiving communion; with singing a hymn the next highest. A key element was the degree of participation they had in the moment. Thus whereas for the congregations their closest moment in the Eucharist itself is the point of receiving the elements, for the Catholic priest it was in the eucharistic prayer when he stands as Christ at the point of the epiclesis when the Spirit is called down, and for the Methodist presbyter the Prayer of Approach. There was a relatively high dependence upon how the minister led worship as to whether people felt connected with God. People made comments that they needed a minister who can 'catch me up in their belief' (Catholic), is good at 'creating an atmosphere in which the Holy Spirit can minister' (Pentecostal) and who can 'put some oomph in it' (Methodist). When comparing the importance of the factors that affected their ability to worship just over 60 per cent said it depended upon who was leading, just over 50 per cent on the sort of service and less than 30 per cent on the other people present.

Through the research process we can conclude that the congregation most likely to experience a closer walk with God in worship is one where the offering is collective by shared tradition and intention; where the empowering comes through good spiritual training; and where minister and people work together. The power of the minister thus lies not just in the way liturgy is conducted – the 'technology of power' – but upon how far they educate and train their people in the understanding of worship, and support lay spiritual development, so that the assembly becomes the primary minister.

That all indicates quite a high level of dependency upon the minister, whether as conductor of or educator about worship, which is perhaps associated with dependency upon God:

> The most popular words used to describe what people most valued about their relationship with God: the two most commonly volunteered things were that they were 'accepted/forgiven' or 'loved' closely followed by God being a 'strength/comfort'. Also high up the list was being 'heard'.

The services researched were all standard forms of their respective traditions. The question is still to be tested in formal research as to whether the more participatory and experimental forms of worship advocated in this chapter do engage people more closely, and whether they do lead to a more liberative and empowering understanding of their faith, but anecdotal experience widely shows that it is so.[5]

Successful house and cell churches and other 'fresh expressions' of church often have more fluid and participatory liturgy which gives more space for lay participation and leadership. These congregations are often growing new Christians who respond to their more charismatic and expressive worship.

Liturgy in conferences is also often experimental and can be a place of powerful God-engagement.

The ordained person's role in developing the liturgy

Let us now look at the process of developing this more rooted form of liturgy, and what the ordained person's role is in that. People are reluctant to take part in the planning of worship not because they are not interested, but because of their lack of confidence in their understanding of what it is about or their fear of getting things wrong. Here trust in the acceptance of our honest, rather than polished, worship by God is important:

Often I would introduce the more collectively planned services on the Sheffield estate described below with an acknowledgement that things might not go perfectly but that was OK as it was about doing our best for God, and that even when it was not perfect, it was acceptable to God.

Also it is useful to stress the sense of listening to the Holy Spirit, and integrating prayer into our planning.

Often people need to be introduced to the idea that worship is a journey or process and that a service should have a shape and sense of destination:[6]

> When I have begun planning services, I have often invited people to consider this like a graph where the height of the vertical axis indicates how upbeat the mood is – where Psalm 66 would be plus one and Psalm 137 minus one. Classic Anglican, Methodist, Baptist and URC liturgy begins at about plus 0.5, dips for a short while to minus 0.2, potters along around plus 0.1 and might get up to plus 0.8 in the post-communion hymn, especially if there is good tea, coffee and cakes to follow. Pentecostal and charismatic worship, by contrast, starts above 0.9, dips to 0.5 and climbs to at least 1.0. There is nothing to stop services being planned to different shapes. We could have a gentle crescendo from beginning to end, or a time of reflective contrition as response to the Word as people maybe make confession followed by an act of commitment to different action.

For several years in the 1990s I was responsible for planning two services a year, involving eight congregations from four denominations across a large out-of-town social housing estate. Each was planned with a different group of about six people, including usually one ordained person. Most of the other lay people generally had no prior experience of planning worship. The clergy role was to be alongside them in creating the ideas and to be the 'orthodoxy backstop' – mine was to enable and orchestrate this process:

> I always began the group in prayer and then asked them to reflect on the questions – sometimes in pairs – What do you think worship is? – What enables you to feel close to God in a service? This opened up all sorts of ideas and helped to begin to connect with this idea of liturgy as a journey and encounter with God. Then I would give some input about the shape and flow of the service and we would discuss what was happening on the estate and in our churches and what

kind of feel or approach we wanted to take in the service. Then we would brainstorm on passages of the Bible that seemed to speak to those themes.

The final services took many forms and would include different types of music and prayers, but those for the week of Prayer for Christian Unity were attended by a growing range of the other denominations and house churches serving the estate. Because Roman Catholics were included, we could not have a eucharistic service but we generally included some symbolic sharing of food either within or at the end of the service, bringing the sacramental closer to the ordinary. The ecumenical nature of the worship gave us a freedom from the set liturgy of any of the four denominations involved, while giving us the richness of all the traditions to tap into:

> One service particularly focused upon the rededication of the congregations to a new phase in mission and to each other. The ordained person in the Planning Group on that occasion was a Catholic and the service was to be held in one of his churches. In the course of our sharing about how his tradition would mark such a process we decided to use the liturgy of 'spurging' (asperging): sprinkling the whole congregation with holy water as a reminder of their baptism. This sort of liturgy was not found in the worship of the other denominations present, and could have seemed very 'foreign'. However, it was in the context of a service that was mostly much more informal than the liturgy from which it was taken, and which included familiar hymns and choruses from their traditions and so it was accepted and valued.
>
> This flexibility allowed God's Spirit to flow both in our planning, and the eventual worship, more fluidly than in much worship. It wasn't the most polished liturgy, but it was very much of the people and their area:
>
> A elderly Catholic layman on another occasion became so caught up in the process that he took over reading the 'leader voice' in the written liturgy at the end of the service, and the person meant to be leading at that point was gracious enough to go with the flow.

This then begs the question: what is the clergy role in the services themselves and what is it when groups within a church conduct worship? Primarily, it is about providing the security for the experimental to be safe. Research on fear has shown that people can cope with pain or the unknown much better if they are literally or emotionally held by a trusted authority figure. The presence of the minister – visible, but not necessarily taking any part in leading the worship – says to the congregation that what happens in the worship is to be trusted and acceptable to God. The minister's presence validates it, and if there are glitches, she or he is there to fill in for a reader who doesn't show up or cope when a disturbed person begins to shout during a talk. This 'holding' role is an essential form of oversight and the more creative the worship is, the more important the minister's confidence in, and endorsement of, the process must be. Saying thank you with a smile when an unconfident reader has stumbled through their first public reading is modelling a God who finds the heartfelt, broken prayer of the publican a more precious thing than the articulate declaration of the Pharisee.

At this juncture let us summarize the points developed in the above sections about this more flexible and shared understanding of worship-leading. The various roles that the clergy need to take are as follows:

- In the initial stages, the ordained person will be publicly and prayerfully 'doing' almost all of the liturgy in a hands-on way.
- As lay people's skills and confidence grow, they will be 'leading', i.e. 'doing' with other people taking an active part in preparation and delivery.
- Eventually, the clergy might simply be 'holding' the service by being present while others are 'doing'.
- Finally, as worship develops to be more frequently held than one person can cover, their role is one of 'making sure' that what others do while they are absent is appropriately and worshipfully done. And not only that these things are done in truth and love but that all that needs to be is done to further God's Kingdom, and celebrate Christ, through the Spirit.

The roles performed by the clergy will also vary with the formality and setting of the services, from the *metaphorical* sacrament of a shared meal at a house or youth group, through formal church services of one denomination to ecumenical services and 'civic' celebrations. The teaching also needs to be adapted to these different settings. These can be encapsulated in Table 8.1.

Table 8.1 Service setting and the ministers' roles

Type of service	Type of 'word'	Type of sacrament	Role of ordained
community fellowship	witness and sharing	faith meal – metaphorical sacrament	making sure
cell/house or youth fellowship	Bible study, theological reflection	agape, faith meal	doing, then leading, then making sure
church (with gathered cluster of cells/fellowships)	preaching, discussion teaching/preaching	agape, love feast, Eucharist	making sure leading, holding
joint service (with cluster of denominational churches)	homily/ multi-media presentation liturgical drama	Eucharist	leading, holding, making sure
public space	multi-media presentation drama, 'mystery' play	festival mass	holding

Practical ideas about making change

All the time in our striving to create good liturgy, we have to test it against the question – what fruit do we want it to bear? The use of a worship band can be because the musicians like playing worship songs or because we feel it will enable people to have a more powerful encounter with God:

> In my research I was struck by the subtle difference in attitude between a singer/guitarist in a Pentecostal worship band and a singer/guitarist who enjoyed leading worship in that way in less charismatic Methodist settings. The first just felt an imperative to praise God through his music; the other wanted the congregation to be less stuffy in their worship. He had not listened to whether they worshipped through their traditional hymns, or whether they felt able to in the worship songs that he liked.

Here we encounter a key dilemma about the role of the incoming minister, who wants to offer something she or he feels is enriching but encounters resistance. It reminds me of the experience of Western, agricultural development workers during the 'green revolution' in India. They found there were four different responses:

- wealthy farmers quickly adopted new strains of rice – they would increase their profits;
- comfortable small family farmers were indifferent – they had enough for their needs;
- subsistence farmers were only just producing enough surplus grain for seed the next year and couldn't risk making any change to what kept them alive;
- the farmers in famine-struck areas were willing to try anything.

Have we a parallel here in congregations?

- big 'successful' churches may say – 'Give us more';
- others say, 'Why should we change? We like what we have';
- beleaguered, remnant congregations that are just about holding on want the safe and familiar;
- the unchurched leading battered fragmenting lives will drink deep of whatever worship helps them see God's life in their brokenness.

Our urban congregations tend to be the latter two. Ellen Clark-King's recent book *Theology by Heart* details her wrestling with the spirituality of inner urban congregations in Newcastle and her own feminist-influenced spirituality.[7] The local women derive comfort and support from the more traditional theologies presented in their churches, and do not want change. Likewise, a Presbyterian minister in Aberdeen spoke to me recently of his small congregation's resistance to the 'weird stuff' and so he felt that indigenized church was only going to be possible by starting parallel initiatives for the unchurched people. However, a small traditional Church of Scotland congregation in a Glasgow estate with a high level of violent death had the imagination to develop a powerful memorial within their sanctuary for those who had died:

> A tree of copper piping has been created, where each dead person whose funeral held there is commemorated by welding a new leaf to it. This tree becomes a focal point for people just to come in and pray.[8]

The congregation were sufficiently open and connected to the reality of lives on their estate that they were able to develop a creative way for linking people bereaved through violent death to their worshipping life. What role had the minister had in that development?

First, she didn't impose her own initial idea, which was a book of remembrance. Second, she had worked with them in a way that enabled them to understand something of the process of theology. Perhaps they had earlier made use of a paper tree and leaves at some other memorial or All Saints' Day service. Third, she was willing to support the congregation in implementing their idea which meant funding congregation members to go on a welding and metalwork course in order to fabricate the tree and be able to fix the leaves. Fourth, the worship space in the church building is sufficiently 'known' to the people who attend the bereavement project based in offices at the back of the re-ordered building, that they feel comfortable going in and spending time there on their own. The worship space is special, but not sacrosanct.

This is in direct contrast to a church in Gateshead which had a similar vision ten years ago of opening its building up for community use:

> Regeneration money paid for re-ordering so that the back end of the space was a two-storey community play facility, and the front remained a rather dark, formal sanctuary. At first, many congregational members volunteered in the children's activities but as the flagship project gained enough money to employ staff this petered out, although the clergyperson remained chair of the project board. The death of a much loved project staff member and her funeral in the church gave a chance to reconnect. Several of the unchurched staff who attended the service were sufficiently affected by it to venture into services for a couple of Sundays, but what they found there made little or no connection with their lives and they soon stopped going. Had the liturgy been less dryly remote from their lives, they might have found continued points of connection.

Finally, how can this sort of contextualized and locally created worship be introduced into a traditional congregation? The two basic alternative approaches to introducing emergent liturgy are: either set up a new service at a different time, or develop an existing one. Neither is best done unilaterally by the clergyperson, as it is unlikely to last beyond the ministry of that person, not being routed through the local people. Winning over the congregation is therefore necessary. The main arguments that often sway conservative members are the evangelistic imperative of reaching the unchurched or persuading the dechurched to return, and bringing greater richness to the members' own spirituality. Change will be strongly resisted unless you can show that what they love and value will also be respected. Often an incremental approach can be taken, which might lead through a very similar set of stages to those outlined above.

A starting place for change to happen and to be accepted by a whole church might be a survey about how to make worship better followed by the establishment of a worship review group. Initially all they might consider is the reading and intercessions rota and what to do about 'special festivals' – Christmas morning family worship and harvest festivals are often the starting places for introducing new things. John Austin talks about this sort of 'liturgy audit'. After some while, that group should themselves be wanting to expand into changing ordinary worship. They (not just the ordained person) then need to undertake consultation with the rest of the congregation. Unless they are truly committed to the new vision, they will not be effective advocates. This is a tough discipline, as it is all too easy to give one's own vision of what will happen when doing the consulting, and not to remain true to the common, agreed one. They can then identify:

1 who are the likely supporters, and how they can be involved in developing the new worship;
2 who are the likely resisters, what are their areas of concern and how can the changes continue to meet their spiritual needs and build them up;
3 which church groups will be most affected by the change a new service or a changed one would bring – and consider whether that will be detrimental to the overall mission of the church and how to involve the affected groups in planning the solutions.

In one setting where I began the process, the following resisters were encountered:

> The choir, which practised in the church before the morning service: as we finally decided to set up an earlier new form of service and worship in the back hall, the choir was not affected. I am not sure how we would have resolved that difficulty if the church sanctuary had been the only space available.

The Church Stewards luckily were on balance in favour of the service, and were therefore willing to take on the extra duty, although this was on rota as a voluntary additional duty for the pilot period. There was some discussion about recruiting more Stewards once the decision was taken to continue the initiative, to lighten the load. Their resistance would have caused a great problem to the project.

The hospitality teams were reassured by our promises to leave everything in the kitchen clean and tidy (and by the fact that we did so!).

We managed to get the practicalities of our impact on the Junior Church mostly sorted out, but we were least successful in this relationship, as once the service did get going the numbers of young people attending Junior Church did drop. What we could have done is instigate a round-table discussion about young people in church and work with the whole church as well as the Junior Church staff to develop a joint programme of young people's activities.

Conclusion

Changing liturgy is about changing our understanding of God at work in our world. Some will be threatened by no longer being able to see God as muffled in a blanket between the pews[9] but an active force demanding our action in the wider world. Others will blossom as their worship strengthens their sense of partnership in God's mission. Any change is hard won and unless a trusted, indigenous leadership group or a clear majority (depending on the ecclesiology) are in favour and get involved, it will not bed in to the culture of the church. But if it is properly introduced and others are trained in the leading and planning of worship, it will grow. The Spirit will be released as people discuss their faith in a richer way. This feeds and sustains the congregation and helps them live their lives faithfully. It also gives people the strength to go out and change their lives and the lives and conditions of others. Worship that trusts the Spirit and lets the real world be wrestled with in the sanctuary nurtures the faith to follow Jesus in spreading the Kingdom outside the church walls.

Notes

1 The city of Vancouver placed the aim of being a city good for all its citizens higher than being a world-class city in economic terms, and has found that economic well-being followed. The people of Sheffield in a survey

conducted by Sheffield First, the Local Strategic Partnership, in early 2005, valued the city most for the friendliness of its people and its green spaces: it remains to be seen whether the planners will follow Vancouver's example. Leonie Sandercock, Professor of Community and Regional Planning at the University of Columbia, has written two books exploring this: *Towards Cosmopolis*, Chichester: Wiley, 1998, and *Cosmopolis II: The Mongrel City in the 21st Century*, London: Continuum, 2003.

2 Ernest, a community activist on a Sheffield estate, came to faith in this way. The estate had benefited from a major regeneration programme, led initially by the rector. As this began to take effect, Ernest said, 'We've got the physical rebuilding, now we need the spiritual regeneration.'

3 For example, *Roots for Worship*, a bi-monthly publication and website, gives ideas for creative worship each Sunday connected to the three-year Revised Common Lectionary (London: Roots for Churches Ltd; <www.rootsontheweb.com>).

4 St Leonard's with St Paul's, Norfolk Park, Sheffield.

5 In the absence of further research, I can only argue from my own sense of when there is powerful God-engagement as I am leading worship and the comments that people make afterwards, and the reports of experimental and creative liturgy from such bodies as the St Hilda Community in London in the 1980s, Women in Theology liturgies during the same period, worship at conferences (which often tends to be more experimental, but which also may be heightened because the people who go to conferences are more spiritually 'tuned in'), one-off services at occasions like the Greenham Common Peace Camp, or house blessings, etc.

6 Tim Stratford explores this more in his chapter.

7 Ellen Clark-King, *Theology by Heart: Women, the Church and God*, Peterborough: Epworth Press, 2004.

8 Reported at the Church of Scotland General Assembly, 2005, Mission Evening.

9 The mystic Meister Eckhart used this image to describe a God who is 'domesticated' within worship.

9

Using worship to negotiate an Action Reflection Cycle

TIM STRATFORD

Many churches' members will have formed a discipline of regular weekly worship. This may well be born out of a sense of spiritual struggle as they seek to become the person they know God wants them to be. That discipline of worship and this sense of spiritual struggle do not always meet each other as well as they might. We go to church in spiritual need and we can come away with that spiritual need only barely touched. Here we will try to offer a fresh approach that takes life's journey seriously. One that is built primarily on an Action Reflection Cycle.

A life of worship

Every time that Matthew, Mark, Luke and John's Jesus meets somebody that they distinguish as a rich or establishment figure, it is with a challenge. Every time that this same Jesus meets somebody who is marginalized, whether that be for physical, economic or spiritual reasons, it is with a healing touch. Those who today claim to be his followers are not always distinguished by the same responses. The Christian Church, after all, is a collection of people who gather not yet fully formed into the Christ-like community that remains their Kingdom hope. The casual visitor who ventures into some churches might be excused for thinking that Christ-likeness is not conceived of as any more than a hope resting in a future new world when heaven and earth finally meet for good. In other places, there is a palpable sense of spiritual refreshment by which people and community are changing.

Collective worship, week after week, provides the opportunity for Christian people to reflect together on who they are, for good and bad, and where they are going. 'What sort of person am I here to be?', 'What does it mean to be the church in this time and place?'

There is a Latin phrase, *Lex orandi – lex credendi*, that means 'the word we pray is the word we believe'. It is often applied to worship by churches that use historic or agreed liturgies. It is sometimes seen as the ultimate purpose of worship but is perhaps a little narrow. Worship is more than words, and can form far more than beliefs. Collective worship gives the church an opportunity to reflect on and amend its very being. Other contributions in this volume provide illustrations of when very significant moments in worship have lent a critical opportunity to recognize change in a particular moment. Here we are going to discuss the 'slow-burn' emergence of insight through a rhythm of worship over months and years.

What follows has been worked out through the experience of Anglican churches in urban areas of England suffering from multiple deprivation. In that sense this description will be limited in its scope but the lessons learnt will undoubtedly be of interest beyond these contexts. This is also limited in that it derives from relatively traditional expressions of church, i.e. churches that gather for worship substantially on a Sunday morning and that have a life of fellowship, prayer, study and community service woven throughout the week. The further application of this understanding to fresh expressions of church leaves countless creative possibilities open.

The Church of England has both a weekly and an annual rhythm of worship that is more or less discernible across its diversity of parishes. The annual rhythm can perhaps be thought of as providing different seasonal overtones through the year; the weekly rhythm is the regular drumbeat that provides structure and shape. This is so, even where the Sunday morning service is not necessarily a Eucharist every week. If there is a further overlying pattern that mixes in family services, morning prayer and baptisms, then it doesn't necessarily cancel out the rest. Providing that the drumbeat of gathering around the Bible in the presence of God goes on, then our weekly rhythm is maintained. Even those who attend just one service a month will recognize the weekly drumbeat and value that the church still meets when they are not there.

The Action Reflection Cycle

Paulo Freire (1921–97) was a Brazilian educationalist whose work since publishing *Pedagogy of the Oppressed*[1] has made a world-wide impact. The theoretical framework he offered has been inspirational to many people involved in community-based education, particularly in urban contexts. At the heart of his thinking is a clear notion of what education is for. Freire demonstrates that education brings power and freedom. He asserts that this should not be for the few because this is simply another form of oppression. The fundamental goal of education can only truly occur in mutuality with others.

This is not the place to offer a detailed analysis of Paulo Freire's pedagogical theories save to say that for churches, particularly those involved in empowerment and liberation among the urban poor, his insights can shine a great deal of light. What we can do in these few pages is apply some of Freire's more practical lessons to the praxis of church life and cycle of worship.

Inspired by his work, others have developed a how-to-do-it method which we might call the Action Reflection Cycle.[2] It is one means towards helping people develop a critical consciousness of their world and bring about change. This cycle can be summarized as a repetitive process of reflection, analysis, decision and action. The action leads to further reflection and analysis. Thus, the problems in which people are caught can be explored and, through practical challenge followed by further reflective exploration, they become ever more deeply understood.

It has been said that Freire's methodology belonged to his own context of revolutionary social change and that it is difficult to translate it into the less-heated contexts of the Western world. Nevertheless there is much that is wrong in Western society but to which people, both powerful and powerless, have become accustomed or blind or accepting. This Action Reflection Cycle can be a means of forming a deep literacy that gives the capacity to read social mores afresh and to provide the motivation to create change.

Within the Christian Church, the light of Scripture can be drawn into Freire's analysis; decisions made in the light of prayer; actions focused sacramentally; and reflection born out of a Christian conscience. It is perhaps no coincidence that historically shaped patterns of worship naturally provide this self-same structure. These patterns lead worshippers to bring their experiences of Christian living into mind and into the presence of God; there to reflect in the light of Scripture; to pray; and to go back to their world prepared to change.

The Anglican *Common Worship* model – a case study

At the turn of the millennium, the Church of England was engaged in a process of liturgical renewal out of which *Common Worship* was born. To some in the church, its liturgies are definitive of worship – the last word. To others, its liturgies provide mere guidance and resources. To both, the written liturgies are only the bones. The flesh and blood of worship are in the spirit of the worshipping community and the lives of its members.

What is interesting about *Common Worship* is its comprehensiveness and general widespread acceptance across a diverse church. What is of further significance to us here is that *Common Worship* offers a very definite, almost Freirean, structure for all its diverse possibilities. Whether you turn to a *Common Worship* wedding service, funeral, Eucharist, or initiation service, the same pattern can be found:

- Gathering
- Word
- Sacrament and Action
- Dismissal.

Some term this the 'eucharistic shape' because it has been most discernible in the Eucharist since the liturgical revision of the 1960s onwards and can be discerned in ancient patterns of eucharistic liturgy. The reason for this pattern embracing the whole gamut of the Church of England's current liturgical diet appears to be primarily missiological. It may be that familiarity with this shape formed by people through their attendance at occasional offices might also help them assimilate what the church is up to in the communion services and other regular Sunday worship. It is a simple structure that people will learn; something that will become part of the liturgical memory.

That this structure is discernible throughout the Church of England's liturgies perhaps points to its significance for regular worship. No matter whether the worship cycle is a weekly Eucharist or a smorgasbord of services, the *Common Worship* structure will be more or less there at each gathering. As it is based on recent normative rites for the Eucharist, it is worth breaking down the ingredients of the 'eucharistic shape' a little further. In *Common Worship* Order One we find that something along the following lines is expected:

The Gathering
Greeting
Prayer of Preparation
Prayers of Penitence
Words or songs of praise
A prayer *collecting* the community's hope for salvation

The Liturgy of the Word
Readings from the Bible
Biblical songs and Psalms
A gospel reading
Spoken reflections applying God's word in the Bible to life in the
    here and now
Declaration of Faith
Prayers of Intercession

The Liturgy of the Sacrament
Sharing a sign of peace
The taking of bread and wine
Eucharistic remembrance
The breaking of the bread
Sharing of bread and wine

The Dismissal
Prayer
Hymn(s)
Blessing
Going (in peace to love and serve the Lord)

Now, this is not cast in concrete and a number of variations are actually offered in the text and in the notes. Nevertheless, this is provided as a normative pattern for regular worship and it claims roots deep in the Western Christian tradition. Undoubtedly, this is a pattern that is replicated in many churches throughout the world.

This eucharistic pattern can all too easily be a predictable running order. This is the way we do things. We arrive at church, we perform this routine and we go home – a religious skeuomorph. The Action

Reflection Cycle provides a key that can unlock its wealth. And a worshipping community whose eyes are opened with this key to the challenges of the words they say each week, and the actions they make, will have the capacity to find both the change and the liberation that are at the heart of the gospel.

Although the structure and possibilities are invariably present in churches for the worship of the people of God to be transformational, there are also fossilizing forces around. When worship is conceived of as a series of separate events, it is harder for the community to learn – the commitments made on one occasion aren't necessarily built on next time. Where spirituality is internalized and only conceived of in individual terms, then there is little reinforcement of fresh insights. Where there is no dialogue, then the word of God is unlikely to be expressed by the minds and mouths of the people. Also, the libratory work of the liturgy can easily be hindered by the cultural accretions that have petrified many church congregations and stopped expression.

In some churches, the starting point to unlocking the liberating and transforming dimensions of worship might mean freeing up the sermon slot from being a 20-minute lecture; in some it will mean reaching out to share peace with neighbours; whereas in other churches it might mean learning to pray for each other's real-world needs. In every case it should be no surprise that the church must change before it can change the world.

A eucharistic cycle

Eucharist is transformative for all who allow themselves to enter into it. The gospels describe the transformative effect on people that occurred in many of the meals that Jesus shared. The last of these meals, and the one we continue to commemorate, was transformative even of Jesus. The gospel writers tell us so.

In two of the synoptic gospels, the Last Supper is recounted between Jesus being anointed at Bethany and predicting Peter's denial on the way to Gethsemane. Luke does not include the story of Jesus being anointed at Bethany here although he does include a note that Judas set out to betray Jesus immediately before Passover. Matthew and Mark use the Bethany story and the waste of perfume to explain Judas' betrayal. John's Gospel does not include a full account of the Last Supper in the same way as the other gospels. He does recount, between the anointing at Bethany and Jesus' prediction of Peter's denial on the way to pray before his arrest, a number of events associated with it, however. These include a prediction of his death, his washing of the disciples' feet prior to the Passover meal and a conversation about his betrayal during the meal at which point Judas leaves. In all four gospels this meal is the galvanizing moment. It is the point at which Jesus faces his future and binds it to the Passover symbols of bread and wine. To this supper, Jesus brings himself and his people's history. In a decisive moment he walks out to his arrest and a sequence of actions that have forever changed our world.

In this supper too there is a transformational moment for Judas. All four of the gospels include a conversation about Jesus' betrayal over the supper table. Matthew and John name Judas. John tells us that Satan entered him as soon as he took the bread. Here we find Judas' hopes and fears are brought together and his action galvanized.

This is also no neutral moment for Peter. Luke tells us that Peter was one of the two disciples who made the preparations for this supper. John tells us that Peter objected to Jesus washing his feet. All four gospels tell us of Jesus predicting Peter's denial of their friendship. To this meal Peter brings his loyalty to Jesus. Peter reaffirms it and follows it up for a little while before eventually letting Jesus down.

The gospel writers do not just randomly offer these events to the church, along with the transformation wrought in other people's lives over a meal table with Jesus. The Last Supper itself occupies such a central point in the gospels that its significance cannot be missed. Here we have a model for the way we might seek transformation in the light of Christ's life for our own lives.

It is in our seeking to make real these transformational possibilities that the Action Reflection Cycle can offer some help. People and congregations can struggle to negotiate the changes in their lives that they long for. They need a paradigm that opens up these possibilities. Eucharist indeed offers this – where the accretions and associations of the ages do not obscure it.

When people struggle to see where they are going, then some interpretation of this paradigm is necessary. There follows an attempt to reconceive the *Common Worship* eucharistic shape in a way that lends some help. Gathering, Liturgy of the Word, Liturgy of the Sacrament and Dismissal suggest a rather two-dimensional social occasion. We gather, we do things together and we leave. It's the sort of thing that could happen in almost any sphere of life, work, play or home. Here, with this Freirean conception we will try to open up purposeful and spiritual dimensions. And we don't need to struggle to do this. This is simply a new way of looking at what churches are already doing. Hopefully, it will bring new insights and can offer a congregation the means to change. We will look at the Eucharist as *Common Worship* has divided it into four sections, but we will relabel these sections, taking away their social descriptions and replacing these with words that describe the Spirit's movement. Figure 9.1 shows the Action Reflection Cycle superimposed on a eucharistic shape.

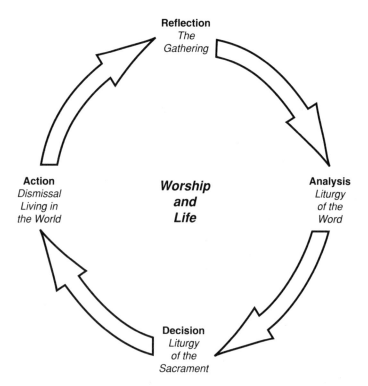

Figure 9.1 The Action Reflection Eucharist

1 Reflection

Our first movement in worship we will call Reflection. Its ingredients are as might be expected:

Greeting
Prayer of Preparation
Prayers of Penitence
Words or songs of praise
A prayer *collecting* the community's hope for salvation

During this time, the congregation are invited to bring the experience of life as it has been lived into the conscious presence of God. Not every liturgical option will necessarily help people with this. Words of greeting such as

In the name of the Father
and of the Son
and of the Holy Spirit.
or
The Lord be with you.
And also with you.

are quite appropriate. More care may be needed over a prayer of preparation. One concern often expressed over the normative *Common Worship* Prayer of Preparation, also known as the Collect for Purity, is that it begins with a plea for cleansing. From time to time, this may be the means by which people want to bring their experience of life before God – but surely not all the time. Thanks and celebration may sometimes be the order of the day. *New Patterns for Worship*[3] offers a wealth of alternatives such as:

God of our days and years,
we set this time apart for you.
Form us in the likeness of Christ
so that our lives may glorify you.
Amen.

The way that the Prayers of Penitence can help people is also clear, bringing their reflections on life as it has been lived in the week or so that has passed. But it may not always be right that people are encouraged to express regret for the past in doing this. Perhaps sometimes they should positively be encouraged to offer celebration. Also, the Prayers of Penitence can provide a powerful way of letting the Word of God shine on the nitty-gritty of life as worship moves from analysis to decision later on in a service. (See also p. 96.) Nevertheless, this normative *Common Worship* pattern of penitence at the start belonging to our reflecting on the past as we gather in the presence of God has some sense about it.

Words and songs of praise will often include something like the Gloria in Excelsis. This is often conceived of as a response to God's forgiveness but it also serves as a reflection on the greatness of God. Other hymns that are chosen for this part of worship ought to pick up some reflective themes on life's journey.

The collects in *Common Worship* are not themed to a particular message carried in the readings as had been true for a while in earlier collections of such prayers. In the seasons, particularly around Easter and Christmas, they pick up a strong flavour consistent with the readings. However, throughout the year, in strong seasons and ordinary time, these collects always have a salvific nature. In the light of people's reflections on where life has taken them, they point to eternity and encourage worshippers to begin their response.

These observations on the liturgy as it is most likely to be encountered demonstrate how the opening of worship can help people begin the Action Reflection Cycle. The very act of gathering in worship demands that people reflect on life as it has been lived. It may be that worshippers simply need to be aware that this movement of their spirit is an attitude they need to foster.

2 Analysis

Next, *Common Worship* would have us move into the Liturgy of the Word. In terms of our Cycle, we might consider this to be analysis. This has a harder edge than the reflection. Here we shine the light of God's word across the rough texture of our lives. The liturgical ingredients might include:

> Readings from the Bible
> Biblical songs and Psalms
> A gospel
> Spoken reflections applying God's word in the Bible to life in the
> here and now
> Declaration of Faith
> Prayers of Intercession

When all of this is led from the pulpit and lectern, some degree of analysis can be achieved. Freire believed that shared power in learning was essential. Education for liberation demanded a forum that was open to the imaginings and free exercise of control by learners and teachers. Participation by congregational members in reading 'lessons' or leading pre-printed prayers is only a nod towards this. Analysis of our world in the light of God's word by a church that is truly learning will best take place where all of the people can take some control. This encourages many modes of using the 'sermon' slot that push the boundaries of traditional expectations. For instance:

- Preaching in dialogue – involving the whole congregation in open discussion and storytelling. This cannot be a question and answer session where the professional preacher knows the answers but something much more risky than that (see *Interactive Preaching*, for more discussion).[4]
- Setting up small circles within the congregation where conversation and storytelling are encouraged. Some groups may have something they want to say to the whole congregation as they re-assemble.
- Pre-prepared statements by people who are carrying burdens, joys or experiences of real life and Christian service that assist people in shining the light of the gospel on themselves.
- Quiet and meditation.

One of the weaknesses of the *Common Worship* eucharistic shape is that the only immediate response to the word of God demanded is the Creed. Such a corporate and agreed statement of common faith is often helpful here. But it may be that sometimes people need to move directly to prayer. It may be that some other form of response is needed: praise, penitence, peace. It is good that people absorb the words of the Nicene Creed into the very bones of their being by weekly repetition. Moving the creed to another point in worship from time to time, though, for the sake of a better response to the word of God, may be of value. The Gathering and Dismissal offer much scope.

Prayers of Intercession seem to be the one moment in the liturgy when the real concerns of local people can be freely expressed to God in the voice of the congregation. Somehow this seems to happen so rarely. Pre-printed books of intercessory resources may perversely be stymieing local creativity and concern. It often seems to be the case that the only contemporary people to be mentioned in parish churches during their intercessions are the Queen, the sick and the dead. Any truthful analysis of the ills of our world in the light of the gospel should throw out a host of intercessory concerns. The ministry of collecting these concerns and expressing them in prayer may be one that urgently needs nurturing.

Using the Liturgy of the Word to engage in some serious analysis of what God's will might be is clearly not without its challenges. To some extent, this analysis will happen even where the challenges are not faced. Where they are, some far more vibrant decisions and actions may come into the realm of possibility.

3 Decision

Next, a congregation is urged into symbolic action from the sharing of signs of peace with one another to the receiving of tokens of Christ's passion. This gives expression to a desire for Christ-like living. Here begins again a commitment to follow in his footsteps. The liturgy will demand:

> Sharing a sign of peace
> The taking of bread and wine
> Eucharistic remembrance
> The breaking of the bread
> Sharing of bread and wine

The sign of peace seems to act as a fulcrum between our Reflection/ Analysis and Decision/Action. At this point the congregation are urged to move from thinking to changing. This exchange finds its roots in Paul's advice to the Corinthian Church about their meetings and commemorations of the Lord's Supper (1 Corinthians 11.17–end). This is the earliest description and advice for Christian eucharistic practice that we have. Even then, we see divisions within their community in need of healing.

In today's Church, such hurts and divisions are equally likely to exist. Perhaps only the church in which there is minimal interpersonal contact may be free of this. Churches whose members are spending their time in ministry, service and fellowship with one another are much more likely to experience conflict. The peace provides a moment in the regular cycle of worship when people may be encouraged to move from reflection on what has been to committed action. Reaching out across potential divisions is an obvious step in preparing for what is ahead, and was a demand Paul made of the Church in Corinth.

The actions of taking bread and wine, remembering, breaking and sharing are explicit means for a community to unite itself with Christ's company. If this seems obvious, remember that it is not necessarily so to every member of the Church. Such exposition happens very rarely and is sometimes confined only to the Confirmation Class.

4 Action

Here the liturgy offers only commission:

> Go in peace to love and serve the Lord.
> *In the name of Christ. Amen.*

Prayer, hymns and blessing may of course give further expression to this. The real action is that which happens in the life of the church in the days to come.

While all of this seems obvious to some, there is not necessarily a guarantee that people who have spent a lifetime shaped by worship and Eucharist share any common understanding of what they are doing. Churches can be divided by little things such as different perceptions of sharing the peace – where some want to hug every member of the congregation and others only want to shake their spouse's hand. There can be equally significant, though perhaps hidden, divisions between those who want to take their communion in a quiet and personal way against those who want to do so in obvious fellowship with those around them. It may be that, for a church beginning to explore more explicitly this Action – Reflection approach to worship, such issues need to be among the first things exposed to the reflection, analysis and possibility of change.

As well as the church being encouraged to give time and under-standing to its practice, some fresh thinking about music and move-ment is required. The gathering hymn might not simply need to help people gather in God's presence but also to recall their response to his beckoning over days gone by. A gradual hymn might need to help people do more than reflect on a message from Scripture but begin some analysis of human actions. During the Eucharist itself, it is worth remembering that people may be engaged in real spiritual struggle and decision. As Kathy Galloway demonstrates, the Iona Community are among those who have been working at hymnody and song dealing with these sorts of themes.

Making worship live

In a relatively small church setting on the edge of Liverpool this understanding of worship has helped to bring some integrity between what the church was about during the week and what it proclaimed on a Sunday. This was a church built among the deep urban deprivation of an outer estate that had set about using its buildings and human resources to enhance life. (I write in the past because having recently moved from that patch it would be presumptuous to assume that things have remained static.)

The first response of that church's key lay leaders as we began to explore worship in these terms was, 'Why has nobody told us this before, it makes sense of it all.' We set about reviewing our worship and experimenting with some of the ideas emerging through the *Common Worship* enterprise. One of the most significant things we did was to relearn how to use the sermon slot as adults together with significant stories to tell.

One of the early and most moving occasions was on a Remembrance Sunday when an older and more conservative member of the congregation was primed to speak of his war-time experiences. We were left in tears. It didn't stop there, however, as another veteran wanted to tell his stories. He was a particularly tough man who had worked most of his life as a prison officer and demanded clear discipline. He had previously condemned our dialogues during worship. His story too left us in tears. Then there was a third. These were real adult stories that met Christian tradition with the hard truths of our own generation's behaviour. That Remembrance Service left a commitment to seek peace which it had been difficult to engender in previous years. This was because it came from the lips of those who had been involved in war themselves. Coming from the minister it could never have been accepted – by the veterans, above all. It would never have had the same authenticity.

This occasion also changed the thinking of some members of the congregation who had very traditional expectations of what should happen during a 'sermon'. The stories told had been the most natural thing of all to do and much more significant than any preaching they were used to.

We soon came to learn that all of our significant stories were not so far in the past. Indeed, we were still living them. Although the congregation was small, 40 or so adults, the church embraced over 20 pieces of project work running through the week. This drew on over a hundred adult volunteers, all of whom understood themselves as belonging to and working with the church. Those small number of volunteers, who were on a spiritual journey that they sought to express in the discipline of regular worship, found they could bring their stories of the weekday ministry to church with them. Here they could reflect and learn and pray and share and change.

I can't argue that every Sunday at the Good Shepherd was what it should have been. But our re-formed understanding of what worship was about kept ministry alive and vibrant. It was a place where difficulties were shared, joys expressed and prayer for what real-life members of the congregation did through the week were offered. And the worshippers brought something extra to the project life of the church that the other volunteers could notice – something from time to time that was expressed in the 'apt liturgies' that Ann Morisy writes about.

Conclusion

The Church of England has offered us an understanding of worship that moves from Gathering to Dismissal. There is a certain universality about this that can't be denied. Students of Freire have offered a model for formational communities that moves from Reflection to Action and to Reflection again. Those who have entered into a discipline of regular Christian worship alongside others may find that reconceptualizing what they are doing in Freire's terms has value. By doing so it is possible to bring an integrity between worship and the rest of life that prevents God's Spirit from being compartmentalized. It changes both worship and the big spaces between times when life is lived outside the church.

While this understanding of worship, like Freire's own model, has been worked out in the context of a poor urban community, it may well have application in other contexts too. Indeed, the most prosperous and powerful may find greater benefit in freeing God's

Spirit from the religious compartment. Exposing the struggles of daily life to the light of the gospel and to prayer as suggested here may be an even more urgent issue elsewhere.

This is no panacea that can be claimed to make all churches live, but this chapter is offered as a learning aid from the urban church that could bring new life to others.

Notes

1 Paulo Freire, *Pedagogy of the Oppressed*, Harmondsworth: Penguin, 1972.
2 The Action Reflection Cycle as it appears here was developed especially for English usage by Laurie Green, in his *Let's Do Theology*, by linking Freire's understandings of liberative education with the work of Joseph Cardijn, Segundo, Joe Holland and Peter Henriot. See p. 24 ff. of *Let's Do Theology*, London: Cassell, 1990.
3 *New Patterns for Worship*, London: Church House Publishing, 2002, p. 40.
4 Tim Stratford, *Interactive Preaching*, Grove Worship Series No. 144.

Index